Living Divine Relationships

Heaven's Library

by Master Zhi Gang Sha

Elite Books

Santa Rosa, CA 95403

www.EliteBooksOnline.com

This book is the first in the series entitled Divine Relationships.

Library of Congress Cataloging-in-Publication Data

Sha, Zhi Gang.

Living divine relationships / by Zhi Gang Sha. — 1st ed.

p. cm.

ISBN-13: 978-1-60023-010-3
ISBN-10: 1-60023-010-5

1. Spirituality. 2. Interpersonal relations — Religious aspects. I. Title.

BL624.S4755 2007

204 — dc22

2006031871

No part of this work is intended to be a substitute for professional medical, pastoral or psychological guidance, advice or treatment.

Typeset in Cochin

Printed in USA

First Edition

10 9 8 7 6 5 4 3 2 1

Heaven's Library
Divine Teaching Series

The purpose of life is to serve. I am a universal servant. You are a universal servant. Everyone and everything is a universal servant. A universal servant offers universal service, including universal love, forgiveness, peace, healing, blessing, harmony and enlightenment.

The universe is divided into the physical world as the yang world and the spiritual world as the yin world. I am a universal servant serving both humanity in the physical world and souls in the spiritual world.

I have three life missions. My first is to teach universal service, empowering people to be unconditional universal servants. The message of universal service is:

I serve humanity and souls in the universe unconditionally.

You serve humanity and souls in the universe unconditionally.

Together, we serve humanity and souls in the universe unconditionally.

My second life mission is to teach healing, empowering people to heal themselves and others. The message of healing is:

I have the power to heal myself.

You have the power to heal yourself.

Together, we have the power to heal the world.

My third life mission is to teach soul wisdom, empowering people to transform their lives and enlighten their souls, minds and bodies. The message of soul wisdom is:

I have the power to transform my life and enlighten my soul, mind and body.

You have the power to transform your life and enlighten your soul, mind and body.

Together, we have the power to transform the world and enlighten humanity and all souls.

My three life missions are to empower people and souls in the universe. The ultimate goal of these three missions is to transform the consciousness of humanity and souls in the universe, in order to join all souls as one to create a harmonized universe.

The beginning of the twenty-first century is Mother Earth's transition period into the Soul Light Era. Natural disasters, tsunamis, hurricanes, earthquakes, floods, drought, extreme temperatures, famine, disease, political and religious wars, terrorism and other such upheavals are part of this transition. Millions of people in Mother Earth are suffering from depression, anxiety, fear, anger, and worry. They suffer from pain, chronic conditions and life-threatening illnesses. Humanity needs help. The consciousness of humanity needs to be transformed. The suffering of humanity needs to be removed.

One of the most pressing needs of humanity and all souls at this time is access to divine wisdom and its gifts of knowledge, insight, love, forgiveness, compassion and peace. Sacred writings have been made available throughout history to pass down heavenly wisdom and knowledge to those who are open to receiving and disseminating it. In past ages, however, the true writings, true wisdom and true sacred knowledge were distorted or diluted to suit the purposes of the cultures, political structures and religious institutions of the time.

Now, much sacred knowledge is flowing to Mother Earth to help raise the consciousness of humanity and all souls. At this historic period, Heaven's Library has been formed under Divine Guidance to assist in this mission. The objective of Heaven's Library is to offer a series of divine teachings that reveal practical divine tools and treasures to empower people to heal and enlighten themselves and others, to transform every aspect of life, and to create a harmonized and enlightened world and universe.

In 2003, I was chosen as a divine servant, vehicle and channel to transmit permanent divine healing and blessing treasures to humanity and souls in the universe. These healings and blessings can be physical, emotional, mental or spiritual, and they cover all aspects of life, including relationships and finances.

The Divine has guided me to transmit particular abilities to selected individuals in order to create Divine Writers for Heaven's Library. They are also called Divine Writing Channels of Zhi Gang Sha. Each is assigned a series of Heaven's Library books to flow in my voice. The titles come from the Divine. Each series and each title is tailor-made for this representative of humanity at this particular time in his or her soul journey. The content also comes from the Divine. The books cover many aspects of life — ancient wisdom, indigenous wisdom, guidance on the life stages of babies, adolescents and adults, music, yoga, business, technology and more. Their primary focus is to deliver soul wisdom, which includes divine love, forgiveness, compassion, intelligence, knowledge and practice on all of these topics.

I have transmitted permanent divine treasures to the Divine Writers to open their divine writing channel and to download the divine books to their souls. Then, after invoking these gifts as they sit to write, they deliver my books by flow. This means the Divine Writing Channels "borrow the mouth and hands" to flow and write out these divine teachings on every aspect of life. They do not use their "logical heads" to think about how to write or what to write. Instead, they call upon the gifts and then write down what they inwardly hear. We also have Divine Editors who have received specialized permanent divine downloads to edit these books. I do a final review and approval. This is how the divine books in Heaven's Library are produced.

The first divine teaching series of Heaven's Library is *Divine Relationships*. The first book in this series is *Living Divine Relationships*. It is flowed by one of my certified Assistant Teachers, Dr. Aubrey Degnan. I thank her for this contribution to the mission. I thank Diana Gold Holland, Lynda Chaplin and Allan Chuck, the Divine Editors who edited this book. I thank Diana Gold Holland and Lynda Chaplin for the book design, and Melissa Knight and Alan McLean for the logo. I thank Lynda Chaplin for the layout. I thank Wei Fu for the technology supporting the first eBook version.

The Divine Teaching Series books produced by Heaven's Library are totally committed universal servants. Open your heart and soul to read these books. Apply the wisdom, knowledge and practice in these books to heal, transform and enlighten your life. Heaven's Library is very honored to announce to all humanity and to all souls in the universe that divine teaching, including divine wisdom, knowledge and practice in every aspect of life, will be revealed and shared in its publications.

Digest it. Absorb it. Apply it. Benefit from it.

I love my heart and soul.

I love all humanity.

Join hearts and souls together.

Love, peace and harmony.

Love, peace and harmony.

These divine teachings will serve you always.

With love and blessing,

Master Zhi Gang Sha

To live in divine relationship, there is only this moment. You must be willing to stand on the edge of the precipice and be in the state of not knowing. This is the giving up of your ego and the opening to the guidance of God. You must come to trust exactly at that point where you are most scared of the unknown. You come to be empty.

Now you are a vessel for God's work.

To be guided by God is to allow the path to open in front of you. It is surrender to the divine unfolding of your life. Once you understand the profundity of this spiritual principle, you may enter the sacred space. This gift of connection abides within your own heart.

Foreword

Living Divine Relationships is presented on this day as the simplest alignment between any soul and the soul of God. This relationship, of the utmost importance, is the relationship between your soul and the soul of God.

Within this relationship is my soul, that of Zhi Gang Sha, as the golden funnel from God's heart to your soul. Bow down with me, for you are a divine servant and vehicle, just as I am a divine servant, vehicle and channel of God, the Creator, the voice of the Divine.

As you open, the Divine will be heard within your mind and your heart. As your soul is filled with humility, the space opens for the golden teachings to be heard. The primary relationship is now in position.

From this alignment, the living relationships will form about you as your spiritual community, as your physical family, as those who come to you seeking healing, your blessing and your teachings. Each of these relationships offers your soul the opportunity of purity and grace in my name as your servant.

I have traveled through countless relationships with each of you who read my books. In this moment, your mind will open and you will see where I have traveled with you. And you will further see what must now become complete, pure and whole.

All living relationships are lessons. All living relationships are moments for the expression of kindness, compassion and the birth of wisdom.

These are my words as your messenger throughout time, throughout the universe, and now throughout the human form on this day in the Soul Light Era. This is the beginning of our time together.

Thank you. Thank you. Thank you.

Master Zhi Gang Sha

Living Divine Relationships

TABLE OF CONTENTS

The Top Divine Relationship
is with God

To realize your soul's purpose upon this planet and in this lifetime, you must practice the three "golden keys:" total obedience, total devotion and total gratitude. To whom? Only to the Divine. This is the essence, quite simply put, of your life purpose.

Once you understand the profundity of this spiritual principle, you may enter the sacred space of living a divine relationship with God.

God, the Divine

To live in sacred relationship is to hold, to cherish, to honor deeply, in each breath, the beauty, the holiness of the connection with God. To be with the Divine in every breath is to be in the golden light blessing of God.

When we live from this connection, this alignment between our soul and the heart of God, we become our highest nature. We directly understand the connectedness between ourselves and the entire universe. We are never alone, never abandoned. We are cherished and held in love in the heart of God.

God is infinite. God is finite. God is beyond our conceptual minds. God is beyond any pictures and statues. God is in everything. God is the Source. God is a faceless and formless presence. God's heart is present at this moment as you read these words. God will come when you call his name.

God travels through brilliant light. God travels through prayer. God arrives in the cry of the infant being born. God is in your soul.

God will speak with you directly. God will guide you. God will give you wisdom teachings. God will wash clean the Akashic Records to help you realize your soul's enlightenment. God will give you many gifts beyond your ordinary thinking.

God speaks with you through your heart. Your heart must open and your mind must empty to become a vessel to hear the words of God. As your heart opens, compassion for all souls enters you, a deep understanding of the struggles of humanity, plants, birds, animals, oceans, rivers, stones …. All forms of life have a soul, and all will have struggles. It is this struggle that you come to see and wish to ease.

As your heart opens, you will hear the messages of God. This is the primary channel through which you will communicate with God. I call this your Message Center, for it is from here that you send and receive communications with God. You "say hello" to God. This is a deep secret. Until now only very high-level teachers have known how to do this. And now I release this information to the public, to all souls, for we are entering a new age in our universe. It is called the "Soul Light Era."

In this Soul Light Era, all souls will have greater access to the Divine, to God's heart and soul. Many may not realize that God has a soul and a heart. Many may not realize that God can subdivide his soul such that aspects of his soul can enter into you.

When God subdivides his soul and that aspect of his soul comes into your physical body, your longevity and health may be restored. When aspects of God's subdivided soul come into your mind, your mind will be illuminated. When aspects of God's subdivided soul come into your heart, your emotions will become balanced. The more positive and pure emotions will become stronger. You will have more gratitude, peace, and compassion.

Let your heart open and guide you, as it is truly God who is guiding you. To be guided by God is to allow the path to open in front of you; it is surrender to the divine unfolding of one's life. It is not following your own plan. Rather, it is allowing the Divine Plan to pick you up and place you "as is" as part of the larger puzzle of your life. To be guided by the Divine is to melt, to be without attachment or preference. To be guided by the Divine is to perceive life as lessons rather than complaints and shortcomings. To be guided by the Divine is to totally let go. It is rather like jumping off a cliff into the unknown. It is waiting for the invitation rather than requesting.

With this softening, your previous concepts and goals begin to shift. Your worldly wealth, the money in your physical bank, will not compare to the true wealth of heavenly wisdom. Once your heart is open, God will teach you directly. You will be taught through your daily life, through the challenges and opportunities that come to you. God will teach you through testing you. God will give you many chances to go beyond where you have gone in prior lifetimes. God will teach you in your dreams. God will help you to make wise decisions. God will fill you with a knowingness that is beyond words. God will show you images. You will hear the voice of God speaking to you.

As part of your being a sincere disciple of God, God will help you cleanse your Akashic Records, the large book that records both the good and bad deeds, actions, thoughts and emotions that pass through you in your thousands upon thousands of lifetimes. God will give you the gift of total cleansing if you but seize the opportunity and overcome the obstacles that attempt to inhibit you.

God will give you many gifts beyond your conceptual, logical, and ordinary thinking. The abilities and blessings that can come from God directly are unlimited, vast and sacred. Only a very few are known to you at this time. You may experience seeing through your Inner Eye, hearing through your mind, feeling the light of golden blessings and the feeling of tingles with heat. This is small compared to the vast abilities and gifts that can be yours.

When you put all this together, your total life — its direction, its commitment, its fulfillment — is way beyond your current journey. It is rather like traveling on a narrow path when you could be using vast freeways, with different aspects of your soul traveling in many directions.

These are only some of the many examples of what it means to be living in a close relationship with God, each day and each minute, in all relationships within your life.

God is first. To be living in divine relationship with God is the absolute top, the ultimate, the highest connection you can realize in this lifetime. It is the top and also the only true relationship possible when your soul seeks total enlightenment. It is the most cherished relationship throughout all cultures and all time.

This ultimate relationship with the Divine is a deep commitment. You must place yourself second and enter into a quality of service to others, a service to all souls in the universe. For some, this means allowing all souls in the entire universe, both the light side and the dark side, to realize their own enlightenment, to enter the heavenly realms, and even beyond all realms, before it is your turn. You become the shepherd guiding God's flock.

The Many Names of God

Because this book is written to help you enter into living in divine relationship with God and all those who are in your life, I will not debate the accuracy of the different spiritual religions available to us on the planet at this time. Holy seekers, yogis, priests and even Sunday worshipers have many names for God. Let us not debate which is best. That is not my purpose here.

God is the presence that each of us knows deeply in our hearts. Songs, poems, books, symphonies, libraries, institutions, churches and many other forms of worship gather around this truth in our hearts to express its own path. What they all have in common is the knowingness that a God exists. Even those who say God does not exist are still speaking in antithesis to something they wish to deny.

God is also known as Emptiness, Adonai, Allah, the Great Spirit, the Tao, Shiva, Oneness, Father, Universal Light, Divine Presence, the Creator, and others. All cultures have their name for God. All cultures have an image of God that is unique to their geography, race and time in history.

Many people recognize the use of light and love as they help others to heal. Priests, bishops, rabbis, shamans and others who preach the name of God throughout many cultures use the words "light and love." Light carries God's presence. Light announces the arrival of God. The many colors of light, the golden light, the brilliant white light, the rays of light, even the light that has no color, the rainbow light and the blue light bring us close to God. We feel God in these qualities of light. Light is also a name for God.

The presence of divine love is also a manifestation of God's heart. The quality of awe and love we feel when holding a newborn infant is our soul recognizing the direct journey this young being has just made from the heart of God. We know this deeper than our words can describe. We know the feeling, the purity of the love from God, as the infant arrives in this physical world. A baby is an expression of the divine love of God.

Divine love can come to us in a moment of peace and comfort as we look at the light of dawn. Divine love can come to us in a thoughtful moment as we reflect upon the wonder and beauty and connectedness of the physical world. We feel uplifted and quiet. We feel the love of Creation. This is also known as divine love.

It is the Creator who brings us to this life and who brings us to these reflective moments, these thoughtful moments when we pause and are consciously close to God. To see the Creator's perfection in the physical world is not a topic for scholars, poets and photographers only. We too see the love, the beauty and the light of this magnificent creation brought to the physical world by God, who is both the Nameless and the One with Many Names.

I am saying to go deeper to the intent in each soul's heart to express this knowingness of the Divine. This knowingness is present in all children. It is often negated and suppressed as the child grows into its early years. Yet this knowingness remains in your heart waiting to be rekindled when you are given permission.

Given permission by whom? From a book, from a friend, and most deeply from your teacher who is a divine servant, vehicle and channel. You are also a divine servant and vehicle. You are a child of God. If you were not in that kind of relationship with God already, you would not recognize the permission or rather the recognition granted you by a kindred soul.

Another name for God is friend. A friend in your daily life may give you that spark that rekindles your love of the Divine and your longing for renewing your relationship with the Divine. A well-intentioned spiritual friend can reaffirm your deepest desire for this connection to again become of the utmost importance to you in this life.

As your heart opens and your mind lets go of its logical thinking, allow the name of God to have many letters and sounds as it travels throughout the universe.

It is true that a sound or a word cannot begin to totally express who God is. So the sound or word is only a small aspect of God. What this sound or word does do is to point in the many directions where we find aspects of God manifesting in the physical world. In the Soul World, as your spiritual channels open, you can travel more fully and completely into the divine presence of God. In this way, you are closer to God than in the physical world.

Yet, while the sound or word is only pointing in the many directions where we find God, there is also something deeper. The sound or word of God, the many names of God that I have used thus far, each carry a soul. They each are a soul. They carry a subdivided soul of God. In this way they are living. And as living subdivided souls of God, when you call out their name, they directly carry your message to God. This is a big secret. It is deep spiritual wisdom. When you say the name of God that is the name you personally use in keeping with your culture or spiritual tradition, you are speaking to God directly.

In this manner, there are many true names for God.

The Meaning of Divine

The divine plane is often seen as separate and much higher than the human plane on Earth. However, this separation is an example

of the kind of limited thinking that the logical mind lo
misguide us. The entire premise of this small book on teacning
living divine relationships is that you, dear reader, can do this, can be
in this quality of relationship while living on this Earth.

So for the impact of these teachings to transform you, you must
now let go of the unconscious habit of perceiving the Divine as different from your life. Yet, know that the Divine is quite different from
the physical life you may be living right now. You can transform your
life, your relationships, your body, your emotions, your thinking,
your very relationship with yourself, and therefore with everyone in
your life, by making these changes:

First, in your heart bring together as one the holy and the mun-
dane. This means to bring together the spiritual world and the physical world as one.

Second, recognize that the meaning of "divine" refers to the heavens, to the celestial. Yet these very words have been written by people
who attempted to separate Heaven and Earth. Know that the time is
now — in the Soul Light Era — to heal these separations while still
understanding their differences.

Third, live each day, each relationship, in the manner that you
know to be of your highest attributes, the very attributes and qualities that you know belong to the highest saints. Place yourself in the
condition of being a saint on this Earth. Live in that way.

Fourth, to be able to truly enter the Divine and the distinction
that makes it different yet not separate from the physical world, you
must first have the foundation of placing yourself in the condition of

being a saint. It is just like you cannot see over the top of any mountain until you first climb the mountain. Then the view is entirely different. Most of humanity is still living and thinking of itself as being at the bottom of the mountain.

But you, reading my words and hearing my teaching, can now enter the space of climbing up the mountain so that you can see the view. This new view is a more accurate view of the entire picture, which includes both the physical world and the spiritual world. To enter into the doorway of the spiritual world, you must stand on this new foundation. This is now the doorway into the heavens, the Soul World, and coming closer to God.

Fifth, move through the doorway of the Divine and fully enter this extraordinary spiritual realm. Divine means "celestial, of the heavens." The souls of the saints, the highest spiritual masters, the angels, the protectors on both the light and dark side live in the heavenly realms. The purest of pure and the darkest of dark live together. They each have a job to do, a task that may take them thousands of years to complete. Then, they too may be sent back to Earth to complete some lessons or task they are given. While they live in the heavenly realm, they may also enter into you by subdividing their souls.

Sixth, to truly transform yourself to become a more divine being, it is necessary that you see and understand more of the celestial realms and the lives and duties of the saints and teachers in these realms. Why? Because with this understanding of the Divine, you can begin to transform yourself while on the physical plane.

This is the purpose of this lifetime, to do this level of transformation, anywhere there is darkness, cloudiness, unbalanced emotions, negative karma, ignorance, attachment, grasping — any ego at all — all of these need to be cleansed and purified. Then you are truly the vessel of pure light, pristine and clear, and able to receive the messages and teachings and duties that the Divine asks of you.

In this manner you too, in this single lifetime, can transform yourself into living a divine relationship with God.

The Meaning of Living with the Divine

I speak to you on this day as a divine servant, vehicle and channel. My relationship with the Divine is that I have the privilege to be a direct channel for God. As a divine servant, vehicle and channel, I can do much more than write these words, even though this is so blessed a service.

As a divine servant, vehicle and channel, my duty is to bring many souls into their soul enlightenment. In order to complete this task that God has given to me, I must be in continual conversation with God.

Thus one meaning of "living with the Divine" is to be in continual conversation with God. I seek his guidance for every life decision that I am called upon to make. I do not question this guidance. I live my life, my relationships with my own family, my business decisions, be they small or large, through receiving this guidance.

So one could say that I do only what this guidance tells me to do. It may look foolish or be difficult to understand from the perspective of the physical world, but from the perspective of the spiritual world, I follow the laws and obey.

In this manner, I am living in divine relationship with God.

There are other qualities of my divine relationship with God that may not show on the outside. Many lifetimes of service to God, in fact even hundreds of lifetimes as a teacher and serious disciple, bring me to this lifetime. My connection with God is so very deep. And many of you reading these words have been with me previously when I have been your spiritual teacher. In this manner, God has trained me and prepared me for the great task of bringing soul enlightenment to all souls in the universe.

It is through these lifetimes of studying and serving God that I have gained much virtue. "Virtue" is a quality that is the coin of wealth in the spiritual world. Just as in the physical world there is money made of paper that is put in the bank and used for all aspects of one's comfort and goals, there is a counterpart to money in the spiritual world. This counterpart is virtue, and it is placed in Heaven's Bank. Virtue that I have accumulated throughout my many lifetimes allows me to give blessings to my students and to all souls.

Virtue is then the means through which I serve God when I give blessings to others. It is far deeper than just being a channel or voice. To give blessings through accumulated virtue is like dispensing the golden liquid that moves through the channel. It is my divine relationship with God that allows me to ask for this golden liquid to flow and then it flows. In this manner, I am living in divine relationship with God.

The ability or gift of manifestation comes through the spirit of God entering into a human form. When God brings an aspect of divine presence to me, it passes through the Soul World at the level of the highest saints. Thus, when I am called upon to manifest a high-level saint, it is both God's wish and the saint's wish to manifest through me. This alignment is essential to manifestation. Alignment of high-level souls is part of living a divine relationship with God. God, as I have said before, is at the top. From this top level in the heavens, the presence of God travels through the many layers of saints, healers, master teachers and guides, and then comes to me in the physical or visible form.

The physical manifestation of the highest saints or buddhas can be seen by students with Third Eye capabilities. These heavenly beings can also be seen by people who have never used their Third Eye. It can happen spontaneously, allowing anyone to see the living presence of a saint.

God can also manifest directly through me when called upon. One of the gifts I am given is to take my students to the heart of God when we are in the sacred space of transmissions. As I said earlier, open your heart to communicate with God. When both my human heart and the hearts of my student are open, together we go to the heart of God.

Thus, I most humbly and honestly tell you the truth. The ability to manifest God is given because of the virtue accumulated through these many lifetimes of service. I am telling you the truth about how this relationship that I have with God works. Even my students who have spent many years with me may not have figured this out.

The power and ability of manifestation is far greater than merely helping things happen in your physical life such as procuring a new job or easing the relationship with a spouse. Manifestation of a saint and manifestation of the heart of God are of a magnitude greater and higher in spiritual capability.

This gift of manifestation comes directly from my divine relationship with God. It is a gift that I have both earned and that has been given to me because of my dedication.

I feel so blessed. I cannot bow down enough as I receive these gifts.

In this manner, I am living in divine relationship with God.

Relationship

As I have told you many times and in many ways, the essence of the matter, the essence and purpose of your soul journey, is to realize enlightenment in this lifetime. There may not be another opportunity like this one for hundreds of lifetimes to come. You know the struggles you go through in this lifetime. Do you wish to continue? *Of course not.* So what can you do? How can the Divine assist you?

These two questions are connected. One is, "What can you, yourself, in this physical form, with your soul, mind and body?" The second is, "How can the Divine help you?" It is said in the Bible, "God helps those who help themselves." This is no secret. The truth is that people read these words and then forget them.

Relationship implies connection. There is a profound relationship between what you can do in this lifetime and what the Divine can do to assist you. This connection is divine Oneness. This relationship of connection is a divine gift. The awareness of this connection is what we struggle to maintain.

Our awareness as human beings is quite faulty. It shifts from knowing we are part of the Divine and feeling gratitude for that awareness to suddenly losing the connection. This loss is a loss of awareness. It is not a loss of connection. The profound truth is that you are always connected with the Divine. God never ever leaves you or abandons you. It is you who abandon God.

When suddenly you lose this connection, this awareness of your relationship with God, you may fall into despair or confusion. I call this "getting lost." I have seen it happen to many people. I have close disciples and students who can get lost. Their egos take over and their soul is no longer the boss. God is still there, I am still there, but it is they who are gone. This is very sad.

When this happens, I always leave the door open. I am a divine servant, vehicle and channel, and in my heart, the door is always open. I never say harsh words because I love those who get lost. People have many lessons to learn. They must go through these lessons in this lifetime and learn what they have not learned before. Then they are ready to rise to a higher level of soul development.

This is the journey. We must all go through it. I had to go through it myself. It was not easy. In fact, it was cruel in many ways, but I prayed to God. Even when my whole family thought I was far gone, I still prayed. I prayed to my teacher. I never turned my back on God, and I always had faith in God to guide me. God was guiding me. God was leading me through experiences so that I would understand the greater picture and be able to help others who struggle like I did. This is called compassion.

So you see it is most important to know that when you lose your awareness of the beauty and perfection of each day and each moment, it is you who are separating from your relationship with God. This is called the "fall from grace." It is not your soul that falls. It is your ego that takes over and convinces you that things are not right. You begin to separate yourself from the perfection and love of the Divine.

I teach my Assistant Teachers and my advanced students to understand this cycle of divine awareness and the fall from grace. I call it "spiritual testing." I tell them that the more they complain, the harder it gets. These are deep spiritual principles.

To complain — and Americans love to do this — is to say to God that there is no perfection. How can there be no perfection? If you will but look closely at this universe, this galaxy, the planets, the Earth, the trees and the sky, at the continual reproduction of divine relationship between all these levels, then you will again appreciate this extraordinary creation of God!

So I tell you this truth: when you get lost, look outside of yourself, look beyond. That's it! That's all.

Look outside of yourself, and you will begin the journey back to the alignment between your soul and the souls of all those around you. This is the Soul Light Era. This means that it is time for all souls to see each other in their divine truth. The truth is that first, ᾿thing has a soul, and second, that each soul is shining divine light. ᾿I told you earlier, divine light is one of the many manifestations and names of the presence of God.

So when you look outside of yourself, you turn your awareness back to others. You will see quite quickly how interconnected all these souls are to each other. If you were to get down on your knees in the forest and look through a microscope at the intricacy and intimacy of each small insect, each grain of dirt, each dead leaf upon the ground, you would be filled with amazement. There is so much life that your usual awareness just passes by.

If you were to go under the ocean and swim with the fish, you would see how the grains of sand move with the tides. You would see the plants under the sea waving with the ocean's currents.

Nobody is alone. This is a profound teaching and a spiritual principle. There is interconnectedness on the microscopic level and on the macroscopic level. Just as the rings move about the planets, just as the sun comes up and the night falls away, everything in the physical universe is interconnected in this same way.

It is said in the Buddhist texts that if you drop a pebble in a still pond, the water will send ripples further and further out. What is the meaning here? It says that you, as the student, are to quietly sit and reflect upon these simple physical laws. In this quiet state, you will see how the universe truly works. You will see with your physical eyes that one simple pebble, or one simple act, or one simple thought, can send ripples out. These ripples go out to the rest of

go out to the bigger pond, the pond of life, of

all is interconnected. This is the meaning of

as I am writing these words today, they are
already touching your soul.

How can it be that my words are already touching your soul?
What I have said so far to you has been about observing the physical universe. You probably already understand these matters within
the physical universe. I merely had to bring your awareness to these
truths that science and thoughtful people know. Because your mind
can understand parts of the physical world, I start with this foundation of knowledge.

Now we must go further. There are many similarities between
the physical world and the spiritual world.

In the Soul World, there are no secrets. All your thoughts and
actions are recorded in the Akashic Records. This is a book in the
Soul World that keeps a complete record of your soul, not only in this
lifetime but in all your lifetimes. So I am speaking here about your
relationship with your own soul, for it is up to you how you wish this
recorded history of your many lifetimes to read.

If, like me, you wish your record of services to be filled with positive words, then you will take great care, each day and each minute,
as to how you live your life. This is so personal. This part is truly up to
you and your soul. This too is a divine relationship because it is a relationship first, given by God, and second, filled with great potential.

Your relationship with your own soul is a bridge between your physical life and your spiritual life. This bridge is the entryway into the Soul World. When you feel the impact of my written words just now, it is your soul that is resonating. Your soul knows the truth of what I am saying. Your soul knows its responsibility.

This responsibility can be as small or as great as you wish. A small responsibility is to purify your own thinking. Never hold anger or complaints against another. Also, be filled with love, compassion, understanding and forgiveness. Now you may think that this is a great task. Yes, to you as a young soul, it is a great task. However, as a soul that is maturing in its soul development, you will quickly recognize what is missing. It is simply to think of others. To be considerate of others, their needs, their well-being is a small- to medium-sized task. Yes, that is true also. But your mind is still limited.

Let me tell you, service is unlimited! Be of service, jump into the fire! We are capable of so much more! The bigger the job you take on, the higher quality of love and thinking you are willing to demand of yourself, the greater the impact you will make upon other souls. This is the pebble in the pond, and this is how it works in the Soul World.

Because in the Soul World time is not linear but eternal, the impact you can make upon the Soul World by merely jumping up several soul levels within yourself is like an explosion of thousands of suns! Yes! You too can be of such great service. Just let your mind use its full potential and be inspired by the possibilities.

There is a connection with the entire planet — with humans, animals and plants — because they all have souls. There is a connection with the heavenly realms where the great saints abide because each of these saints wishes for your soul to join them and be of higher service.

Your inspiration will carry you to the heavenly realms because this is your soul soaring and traveling back to the Source from which we have all come. Inspiration and creativity are manifestations of your soul as well as the soul of God. Do you not think God was inspired as he created this wondrous universe? Remember, many know God as the Creator. Creativity is what the Creator does.

This is God's divine relationship with all of us: he created us. Honor God by creating beauty in your world, your home and your life. Honor God by creating harmony. Look again at the harmony in the forests and the oceans. Create this harmony and beauty inside your mind and it will be reflected also in your soul.

This is the true healing of our soul, mind and body. It is a healing by living with the Divine, by living with this holy example of possibility and inspiration. Bring it into your physical life. Bring it into your emotional life. Live it in your soul. In this manner, you will be living with God and fulfilling part of your task in this lifetime.

It is all about relationship: with God, with me, Zhi Gang Sha, with yourself, with the physical world, with all souls, with inspiration.

Together, my soul and your soul, we have a big job to do. Our task is to bring enlightenment to this universe. To do this, you must prepare yourself. Purify yourself. See the vision. Work hard. You can do it!

I can hear each of you asking, "How? Where do I start?" I hear your questions and doubts, the limitations coming from your mind. I tell you a simple truth. Do not worry. Just open yourself in your heart. Feel the connection you have with me right now. Feel the warmth and the love. This is the love coming from God.

This love comes from God to your heart. Open and receive. Know that you are guided to this moment. Know that all the struggles you have gone through were lessons to get you to this moment. Know that your soul has this moment brought you to the door. The door is this book.

Let me summarize what you have gained in this short chapter, for it is the foundation of the rest of our work. Align your soul with the Divine. Allow me to be the golden funnel from your heart to God's heart. Observe the interconnectedness of the physical realm. Realize that the same interconnectedness is also in the Soul Realm. Greet all moments for the rest of your life with purity, kindness and gratitude. Understand that each of these simple thoughts is reflecting how to live a relationship with the Divine.

Live with this simplicity.

2

The Second Most Important Divine Relationship is with Your Shi Fu

What is a Shi Fu?

As a divine servant, vehicle and channel, it is my duty to help you gain the wisdom, gain the power, gain the virtue that can come to you in this lifetime. This is why I am revealing to you these spiritual principles that have been kept secret for thousands of years. It is a big task. I need you to understand because it will become your task as well. Your task will be to assist me, to do your job to assist all souls in gaining this wisdom at this time of the Soul Light Era.

The wisdom in this chapter will help you understand even further, even deeper, your place in the spiritual world. In the first chapter, I told you about your alignment with God and with your own soul. I told you how the laws of the physical world and the spiritual world have much in common.

Just as in the physical world many of you have chosen teachers or guides or dear friends to help show you the way in your daily life, there is also a guide in the spiritual world just for you.

A Shi Fu is your personal guide or saint. In the Soul World, there are special saints whose duty is to assist, guide, watch over, and speak with the souls of humans on Earth. They have been assigned an important task by the heavenly realm. Some of these great saints are already known to you.

The entire world knows of Jesus and Mary. Many know of Saint Francis of Assisi. Many know of Avoloketeshvara or Guan Yin, now called Ling Hui Sheng Shi. Many know of Ar Mi Tuo Fuo or Amitabha. Each of these great saints is here to protect you during your journey. They have each taken a vow, a very serious vow, to protect you or to show you the way. Each in his or her own way is a manifestation of great virtues. They set examples for you of kindness, healing, and service. They assist you when you are in trouble, and at the time of your death, they will come and pick you up to help your soul travel out of your body and into another lifetime.

On Earth, there are many special days when these saints are honored and remembered. While it is good to honor them, this is not nearly enough. Why? Because as you open your spiritual channels, you will understand even further. The truth is that these great saints are always on duty, always present and doing their job. To remember them once a year or even once a week is not enough.

You must remember them each day, throughout the day. In this manner, you are living in divine relationship with your Shi Fu. In this manner, you are living in divine relationship with all saints. In this manner, you are living in divine relationship with God. Always remember this alignment. God is the top, the highest. Your Shi Fu is second to the highest. Why? Because your Shi Fu is a direct channel to God.

Think how blessed you are to have such a possibility — a direct conversation with a personal high-level saint who is watching over the journey of your soul! This conversation is holy and sacred. Whenever you stumble in life, you can call on your Shi Fu to help you realign with the Divine. In this manner, you are always safe, loved, and even cherished. Your soul can drink of the highest wisdom in the entire universe. This conversation will feed your soul and guide it.

Open your Third Eye! Now! Can you not see the thousands of golden cords of light that connect all saints with all souls in the entire universe? Can you see this exquisite and beautiful tapestry of blessed light? Let me share with you as your messenger.

In the space between our planet Earth and the vast Heaven, there are thousands of saints seated in a holy circle of light. Out of their hearts come cords of pure golden light that curve and weave throughout the space of the sky. One of the precious cords comes down into your heart, into the center of your chest. Inside your heart is a beautiful open flower. The pollen in the center of the flower is fed by this golden cord from your Shi Fu. It is so very sweet. It is pure. It is always flowing.

All you must do is to open your hearts. In this manner, you are living in divine relationship with your Shi Fu.

As you open further, you will understand that these golden cords are beams of light that come from your soul and travel to all souls in the universe. This will come to you in time, for this is the Soul Light Era.

Your Shi Fu is a messenger of light. Your Shi Fu lives in the Soul World at this time. It is, however, possible for your Shi Fu to gain an aspect of physical form. Your Shi Fu can subdivide his or her soul so that an aspect of this saint enters into you. Were this to occur for you, you would be at a very high level of soul development. You would be chosen for a most special job. You would be living as a most pure being while on this planet. You would have transformed many aspects of yourself for this possibility to become a reality.

This may be beyond your imagination, beyond your cognitive, logical mind, but I am telling you the truth. Your potential is way beyond what your small mind thinks. That is why there is a big mind that is the mind of God. At this time, I wish you to know a small part of the possibilities open to you. That is why I tell you this: as you transform your body, each organ and each cell, further into light, you are becoming a more divine human being while still on this Earth. When you cleanse your physical body in this way, you are able to be a vessel of divine light for your Shi Fu to enter as part of his or her subdivided soul.

You must also be able to cleanse your mind of all negative thinking. You must also be cleansed of past or current karma. Your emotions must be balanced. Each of these parts of your body, mind, and soul must be purified. This takes much work. I can show you how in these precious books that I am preparing for you. Do this work with a pure heart, and you can transform yourself in this lifetime. Then, you and your Shi Fu can act as one on this Earth.

How exciting! Does this not touch your heart? Of course it does. Because now you are beginning to understand what you can become in this lifetime. Your soul yearns for the opportunity to grow. Your soul yearns for the opportunity to be of service. Your soul yearns for the opportunity to lead a meaningful life.

Think of your Shi Fu as a partner, someone who opens the door into the Soul World. Think of your Shi Fu as someone who enters into you, and become the door into the physical world for your Shi Fu. This is the intimacy of this holy connection.

This is living in divine relationship with your Shi Fu.

How Do I Find My Shi Fu?

In a word, "yearning." My words touch your heart. It is your heart that is yearning for a connection that is eternal and unconditional. The wisdom in your heart seeks the blessing of pure love that you know exists, and you are searching for this.

This is why you pray. This is why you bow down. It is deeper than showing respect because it is the eternal yearning to go home to the Divine love you have already known. You pray, asking for this love. Our hearts open when we feel this love. We melt all attachments and separation when we are in the blessed state of divine love. This is the yearning that moves us.

To find your Shi Fu, you must first reach out from the depth of your soul and the openness of your heart. Have the courage to stand in the nakedness of your soul, yearning and asking. Have the courage to admit fully how very much you seek the eternal love of the Divine.

Once you truly allow yourself to be in this heart-felt and genuine yearning, you are entering the doorway.

This is but a taste of devotion.

In this yearning and devoted state, bow down. Put your head to the floor. Be humble. Now raise yourself up so you are on your knees and place your hands in front of your heart in the prayer position. Do not be afraid to pray in this manner. It is very important that you show the Soul World your devotion and respect. If you do not, why would they bother to listen to you? I tell you this very directly because it is true. You must show your respect.

Say these words, "Dear God and Heaven's Team, I bow down. I honor you. I love you. Could you please help me and guide my soul to find my Shi Fu? I am very grateful and appreciative. Thank you. Thank you. Thank you."

Remember what I have said to you about being in the nakedness of your soul, yearning and asking for this eternal connection and for this personal guidance. Do not think you can just bow down with your physical body. You must also be bowing down with your heart and your soul. Don't you know that the Soul World can tell the difference?

This is the first step. This is what your attitude should be as you enter into prayer.

Next, ask yourself why you wish to have a personal Shi Fu. Is it to gain soul wisdom, to ask questions about your own life, to seek help for your business or home? These are good reasons. But I tell you seriously, they are also selfish. This kind of attitude will not bring a Shi Fu to you. The saints will simply not even hear you calling out to them. They will not come. The saints are very busy and have many tasks they are doing. Why would they answer requests that are for your own benefit only? This is wrong thinking.

Start thinking of others. Think outside yourself. Look at the world around you. Look at the suffering and darkness and pain of others. Does their struggle not touch you? Do you not wish to make it better? If you knew how to make it better, would you not do it? If you could change the darkness into light, would you not do it?

Ask yourself, "How? How can I make a difference in this world?" This is the way to think. Think of others. Think of the service you can offer with the guidance of a Shi Fu. This is the way to think.

This is the second step. This is your mind becoming more pure as you enter into prayer.

Place these thoughts of service into your prayer. Allow your mind to open into inspiration. Think of how the world, the planet, and the entire universe could be of light. Think of the many ways that beauty, love and peace could show in the entire universe when you are inspired. Be of an inspired mind as you pray. Let the images flow. In this way, you are forgetting yourself and you are now offering yourself to be of service.

It is here, in this very moment, the moment of inspiration, that the saints can see your intention. They can see you wishing to join with them in the tasks they are performing in the Soul World. You are now heading in the same direction. This is an aligning with the purpose of the Soul World.

The third step is the job of your teacher. As a spiritual master, I have helped many sincere and devoted students to find their Shi Fu. When I call out to the Soul World, they listen to me because of the hundreds and thousands of lifetimes I have served them. What I am telling you today is how you too can serve them. I am known to these saints as I have been with them many, many times. This is how I can serve you. I can introduce you.

This is an example of how the physical world and the Soul World have similar laws. In the physical world, a person in a high-level position will acknowledge a personal introduction that is done by someone who is also in a high-level position. It is the same in the spiritual world. You have to get the attention of the saints to make an introduction.

In the physical world, money talks. In the spiritual world, virtue talks. My virtue allows me to gain the ear of the saints when I go to them with a request for a Shi Fu for my devoted student.

The fourth step is in the spiritual world.

I talk to God, and God helps me find the correct Shi Fu for you. "How does this happen?" you may wonder. I will go deeper.

To become a saint, a soul has gone through much. The saints have struggled for thousands of lifetimes in many forms, not just on planet Earth. Yet within them was such a profound yearning, such a profound devotion to God, such a clear commitment to service, that these qualities, like a powerful magnet, guided them to enlightenment.

The saints have succeeded in fulfilling the highest purpose in the journey of the soul. The very qualities that you must have in your hearts as you bow down are the very qualities these saints have cultivated for thousands of lifetimes — not with just twenty minutes of prayer a day. Think of the commitment, the devotion and purity! You will be amazed!

These saints have great individuality. They each have particular qualities they have perfected, qualities that are unique to them and that have brought them to the point of being given specific tasks to perform in the universe. The qualities they have perfected are the same qualities that you must also perfect. So the matching of a devoted student with a Shi Fu is the matching up of similar qualities to be perfected. Once these qualities are perfected in you over many more lifetimes to come, you will have an opportunity to become a saint doing similar tasks to those of your Shi Fu now.

Keep in mind that you may quickly realize this sainthood — even within this lifetime. This has not been heard of by the public until now, but now is such a special time.

Because of the matching of these special qualities, your Shi Fu chooses you. God gives approval. I carry the message.

That's it.

Now I know that many of you reading this book may never meet me in person. So you may be asking, "How can I find my Shi Fu?" You can.

It may be better if you can find me personally to help make this connection. However, if that is not possible, you still can find your Shi Fu in this way.

Follow all the steps I have written. When you come to the third step involving my role as a teacher, call directly upon my soul to help you. Take this precious book that has my subdivided soul within it and place it between your palms as you do your prayer. Call upon God to help you at this point again.

Open your heart to hear the answer as it comes with the name of your Shi Fu. Be careful to listen and believe the first response only. This is important because the second or third response may be the games of your ego and not the direct voice of God. Be brave and allow yourself to accept the name and identification of your saint. Allow yourself to be blessed in this manner. Receive the love of God and this precious connection with your Shi Fu.

Always say *thank you* three times in closing.

There is much more to be said about this divine relationship and why your Shi Fu is your Shi Fu.

Living a Divine Relationship with My Shi Fu

The actual relationship between your soul and your Shi Fu is most holy and sacred. It is holy because it is of the heavens. It is sacred because it is part of the most treasured aspects of the Divine and is to be treated accordingly. "Holy" is being part of the whole, the Oneness. It is our direct connection to the Oneness through our saint, our special guide, our Shi Fu. "Sacred" implies being treated in a most special manner, with care and devotion.

Treating this relationship as sacred does not imply that any other relationship does not have the same potential. Indeed, this is a vast discussion that is the purpose of this entire series of books. Yet, for us as mere human beings, we must start at the beginning. This "beginning" means starting where you can understand the foundation of this work. This means starting with what you are familiar with.

You can probably understand treating a saint as sacred, but can you understand treating your spouse in the same manner? You will in time. Yet to relate to a saint is something you know about, even if you do it only once a week in church, or at the beginning of a meal when you give thanks.

Your task as part of living a divine relationship with your Shi Fu is to be always in sacred awareness. Developing this awareness means to place in the front of your mind the attention and focus of the sacred. Every word, every action, every emotion, every thought is to be practiced as if your Shi Fu were at your side, watching and recording, observing and evaluating, because the degree to which you cultivate an awareness of the sacred is the degree to which you can lead your life accordingly. First is the awareness.

This is most important because your Shi Fu has a greater potential of truly manifesting in you when you are ready. To be ready implies you have done much work and received much blessing.

Your Shi Fu can come to you occasionally, as in a visit. You can gain much in this quality of relationship. Most people know about this and these days, quite a few have experienced it. People call it a vision or a channeling. It happens and then it is done. They return to their usual lives. These moments are but a taste of a Shi Fu knocking at your soul saying, "Wake up! I am here to teach you." This is a fairly low-level connection with the spiritual world. It is sporadic.

Many people have witnessed this sporadic nature in those who identify themselves as teachers. Then these people feel disappointed when their teacher falls out of connection and shows some human frailties. People use these lapses as an opportunity to complain or to criticize. Unfortunately, they do not understand the deeper process that is occurring in their teacher.

Teachers grow and transform. This transformation is what people are witnessing when a teacher has a sporadic connection with the saints and then falls out of connection. Secondly, the very people who complain or criticize are hurting their own growth because their thoughts are less than compassionate. It is a statement about the level of consciousness that the student has attained.

Therefore it is necessary to view this process of sporadic connection as the beginning stages of being in divine relationship with a Shi Fu.

Let us jump into the next levels.

But first, I must introduce the spiritual principle of "levels of soul development." In the spiritual world, there are more than a hundred distinct levels of soul development. Each level is progressively more difficult to realize and attain.

We are born into a level because of the prior journey of our soul. Within this lifetime, we have the possibility of moving to higher levels. We do this by cultivating certain qualities and building virtue through the giving of service to others. We may realize the first stage of enlightenment, soul enlightenment. After this, our soul can move to the level of master or teacher or even higher.

Within each level, greater purity and compassion can be observed from the outside by a friend or family member. As we rise to higher levels of soul development, the vessel of our humanity is purified. We are preparing to be a vessel of light and love. We are preparing to be in communion with the Soul World beyond our connection through holidays, prayers, retreats, meditations or any other sporadic connection.

To enter into a divine relationship with a Shi Fu is to be continually connected and aware that you are connected. Each moment you start to fall out of a pure state, you disconnect from your soul and add qualities to your soul life that will take more work to overcome.

So what am I teaching here? I am telling you clearly this simple truth. You must purify your soul, mind and body to live in direct connection with your Shi Fu. You must also be able to sustain this connection. Then, and only then, are you living a divine relationship with your Shi Fu.

I will now tell you what this sacred relationship means. Living a divine relationship with your Shi Fu is living a quality of life while yet on Earth that is most extraordinary. It is beyond imagination. You become your Shi Fu. You enter into what I call the "hero condition."

You are your Shi Fu. You think like your Shi Fu thinks. You feel like your Shi Fu feels. You see the world in the way your Shi Fu sees it. Your perception is so deep and your understanding is so subtle. Your compassion is infinite. Your clarity reaches backward in time and forward into the future. Your human veins pump the vitality of your Shi Fu. Your brain cells vibrate at Heaven's frequency. God sits in your heart because your Shi Fu's heart and God's heart are already one.

This is beyond immortality. This is sainthood. You are transforming into a saint.

From the perspective of your Shi Fu, there is also a divine relationship with you. There are two sides to this coin. Your Shi Fu needs a human body to continue to learn its lessons. Your Shi Fu needs a human body to experience the human condition. How else can your Shi Fu do his or her job without remembering the suffering and dilemmas of being human?

Your Shi Fu needs this doorway into humanity to continue to serve both on the level of the Soul World and on the level of the physical world. Your Shi Fu needs this connection to do its job. Your Shi Fu needs this journey to the Earth plane.

Thus far, I have shared with you two perspectives on living in divine relationship with your Shi Fu. "Perspective" means seeing something from a certain place. It does not mean all of the reality. Keep in mind that what I am saying here is only a part of the complete reality. As your soul grows, you will be able to see other perspectives.

The two perspectives I have spoken of are the physical and that of the Soul World. First, in the physical world, you are in your human body and your Shi Fu enters into your fully cleansed and pure vessel. This is a quality of partnership and profound connection. The second perspective is your Shi Fu's perspective in the Soul World. Here your Shi Fu needs your physical form, your humanness to remind him or her of the human struggle. You are now a vehicle for the Shi Fu to deepen his or her own understanding of the lessons to be experienced. One could say you are the food enabling your Shi Fu to learn further. This is also a partnership from the perspective of the Shi Fu.

So these are the two perspectives, depending upon where you are standing: in the physical world or in the Soul World, inside your human body or inside the Shi Fu's spiritual body.

Open your minds. Go further. This is low-level thinking because there is still a separation between the physical and spiritual worlds. In fact, when you realize, when you remember, there is no separation. Given that there is no separation in the enlightened mind, in the ultimate truth of this universe, how then can you and your Shi Fu live in divine relationship? If you are mistakenly viewing this relationship as either on the spiritual plane or on the physical plane, where in ultimate reality is this relationship taking place?

In the heart of God sits the origin of all creation. This great vastness filled with love and inspiration created a swirling mass of movement with golden light. As it swirled and swirled, light rays that look like waves rippled out into the universe. These waves of light of the original creation began to quietly consolidate into different particles, both in form and formless, into space and time, into no space and no time, into many dimensions and realities. Each wave of light and movement began to quiet and subdivide into infinite tiny moments of uniqueness.

This uniqueness exists only momentarily and then rejoins the ultimate moving mass of light and swirling particles. Each form becomes formless in all dimensions and then reforms. The element of time shifts as only one of the characteristics of each particle in each dimension. Countless elements of time exist, including that which appears timeless because it is eternal. All dimensions and all possibilities that are limitless co-exist.

Our entire universe with its multitudes of galaxies is only a momentary characteristic of a particle of this vast movement of swirling light wave. All this simultaneously abides in the heart of God. All this simultaneously is the heart of God …. The light, the infinite, the movement, the swirling, the creation, the changing, all of this is simultaneously moving into us and through us as it is in the entire universe and all dimensions.

These are the timeless spaces you can directly enter when your Shi Fu joins with you and the two of you travel to the heart of God. Fly through his universes with your soul. Use the wisdom of your Shi Fu to guide you. Directly experience beyond this universe. Go to the origins, where time and light are one before they divide into their own particles of creation.

Why travel to the heart of God? Once you enter the heart of God and know within your own soul this reality, your soul has jumped into a larger and higher consciousness. From the perspective of the heart of God, can you not see and know more than merely inside your human body and mind? Your Shi Fu exists in a realm that is more closely connected to the heart of God in an ongoing manner. That is why your Shi Fu can help you to enter this exquisite and sacred space.

This then is the third perspective, a divine perspective of total union of the spiritual and physical worlds in the heart of God.

This is living a divine relationship with your Shi Fu.

Because a Shi Fu is a saint, and only a saint, always remember God. A Shi Fu has worked very hard for countless lifetimes in many realms to gain sainthood. This is far more difficult than it is for a human being to realize enlightenment. Enlightenment is but a doorway. So we have a long way to go and that is why I say, "Always remember God."

So let us now bring to the physical world and into your daily world these heavenly perspectives. To enter the physical world, our mind begins to contract and become smaller. You can feel it happen because that is the human condition.

Yet your mind also has the freedom to soar and be open wide. Try to keep the vast open mind in your daily life and all your interactions. How? If you but direct your mind to your Shi Fu and to the journey to the heart of God, your physical mind will stay open. This is what we mean by "remember."

When you look into the eyes of another human being, "remember" that you are your Shi Fu and you know how to recall the heart of God. It is that simple. Do this and you will observe your own perspective about the person in front of you changing. You will see him or her as a particle of the golden swirling movement from the heart of God. You will see his or her divinity because you have within your own mind a profound partnership with your Shi Fu and with God.

When you feel torn and have strife in your heart, "remember" your connection with your Shi Fu. Become your Shi Fu. Use the mind and soul of your Shi Fu to look again at what you thought was a struggle. From the perspective of your Shi Fu, things will look different. Interesting! It is the same situation you are looking upon, but notice how very different it seems when you use the mind and heart of your Shi Fu.

Now shift again, use the mind and heart of your Shi Fu, and go to the heart of God together. Look again at what you called "a struggle," and you will see the same situation in yet another totally different way. Struggles are separations. When viewing from the heart of God and when viewing from the mind and heart of your Shi Fu, struggles melt and creative options emerge.

Your mind can now ask, "What is the lesson in front of me right now?" Inside, a doorway opens and you become freer of your own karma because you are learning that which you must learn as part of this lifetime.

These are ways in which you can use your relationship with your Shi Fu while leading a human life.

But there is more. There is a far greater purpose for this partnership with your Shi Fu than easing your human struggles. The greater purpose is to totally transform your soul, mind and body. Your Shi Fu is the agent, the vehicle for this transformation. To truly soar through the heavens in partnership and in union with your Shi Fu, you must transform yourself.

Every time you think of your Shi Fu or pray to your Shi Fu, your Shi Fu enters you. Each time this happens, you are transformed a little bit more. Each cell becomes a little more light and clean. It is a cumulative process, and that is why we practice, chant, and receive blessings. We need many blessings. We need to chant whenever we can. We need to pray whenever we wish for a connection with the heavens or the Soul World or God. This is our job. We have to work hard.

The deeper we transform, the more able we are to sustain the "hero condition." This is the condition where we become one with our Shi Fu. Live your life with your Shi Fu inside your heart. In this manner, you are living a divine relationship with the qualities of your Shi Fu inside you. You are becoming your Shi Fu.

Past Lifetimes with My Shi Fu

A very long time ago, there was a school where people sat on the ground in a sacred circle. You were part of that circle. I know this because I was there also. The circle was to show the unity and the respect we are to have for one another. It was within this circle that we took a deep vow. We prayed and sang to the heavens as the meteors were falling with fireballs behind them. We witnessed the skies filled with ash and dust. We saw the changes of destruction in the sky. This led us to come together to pray in this circle.

Since that time, we have all gone our ways. Some of us made it to the heavenly realms and some of us became animals and some of us became humans. The vow we took was sacred. Those of us who became animals have forgotten that vow. Those of us who became humans have the opportunity to remember that vow. Those of us who abide in the heavenly realm remember that vow.

The vow was taken because we were in deep thought as we sat in this circle a long time ago. Each of us spoke in that circle. That is why it was a school — because we were teaching each other great wisdom. Many of us had come from the heavenly realms to meet and discuss the great disasters and creation that were coming to this universe.

In times of great change we come together. We share our wisdom and we take a vow. When we sit in the circle and take a vow, there is great power in this show of unity. That power will carry us for thousands of years. That vow was to bring peace.

You may now remember this circle, the debris in the sky and the Earth trembling. You may now remember your conviction and wholeheartedness as you made a vow to bring peace to this universe.

As part of this vow we promised each other to reappear in front of one another, in every lifetime. This is a way to strengthen our connection. We are a group living in a divine connection that is invisible. It is now time for you to remember the countless times in past lives that we have come together.

If I come to you as an animal, it is still me. If I come to you as a brother, it is still me. If I come to you as your mother, it is still me. If I come to you as a saint, it is still me. Think back, and you will open your mind to remember. Each of us in that circle paired up with another. That pair continues to reappear to each other through countless lifetimes.

What does this mean? There are many levels here for you to understand. The first is that there is a reoccurring partnership between yourself and another who was present in that circle. This is a holy and sacred partnership.

Secondly, know that your individual saint, your Shi Fu in this lifetime, has also been your Shi Fu, brother, mother, pet, and saint before. This is not the first time you have met. Your Shi Fu has been living in a divine relationship with you many, many times.

And the third meaning is most special to our time in this life. At this time, there is an even more serious challenge for you and your Shi Fu. "How is that?" you may ask. Because this is a time of ushering in a new age. The vow to bring peace to the universe is now. The conjunction between many planets, between the light and the dark side in the Soul World, the coming of a new age, the ripening of karma of those in the sacred circle is unique to these twenty years.

Your past lives with your Shi Fu each contained lessons and preparations for the task at hand.

And it is deeper than what I have just told you. This special time of the conjunction of so many aspects of the universe offers a doorway to an entirely different way of life within both the physical and spiritual worlds.

If you fail, and I speak firmly and directly here with words that may seem harsh and yet are the truth, if you fail to completely meet this vow that we all made together, you, I, and all of us will have to return to the lowest level in the Soul World for countless millennia.

This is a most serious moment.

More Than One Shi Fu

Each time your soul jumps to a new level, your potential abilities increase. As you grow, so do your spiritual powers. Jumping to a new level is a quality that makes you more attractive to the Soul World. They see a genuine and serious attempt to become a more pure servant for the entire universe and beyond, and the Soul World approves.

In the Soul World, many saints are watching the serious students on the inner journey to see at what point you may be of help to them and their tasks. So as you progress in the physical world, you can become more desirable as a helper or servant to the Soul World, and in particular to the higher saints.

A lower-level soul can pray and pray and never be heard by the higher saints. They are busy. I am sorry to tell you this, but it is true. A lower-level soul does not have the coin of the realm in the Soul World and cannot get the attention of a high-level saint. This coin of the realm is virtue accumulated through service. A low-level soul has not performed enough service for others, has not given enough or helped enough or cared enough. Therefore, this low-level soul does not have enough virtue built up for the Soul World to listen to him.

However, a higher-level soul in the physical world, a person who has performed service, prayer, and acts of kindness and goodness for others will have accumulated much greater merit. This kind of soul has a better chance of being heard by the Soul World and, in particular, of being heard by the saints.

So if you are a higher-level soul, the saints will pay attention. They will watch your progress. They will see you as someone with whom they wish to have a conversation. From their perspective, you may have value and be able to help them in doing their job.

Each of these high-level saints has perfected particular qualities. If they see that you too have similar qualities to perfect, they may begin to come to visit you. For example, if you have a very kind heart, Guan Yin (Ling Hui Sheng Shi / Avoloketeshvara) may begin to visit you. If you have a love of wisdom teachings, then Wen Zhou Fuo (Manjushri) may come to visit you. If you wish to perfect your skills in the healing of others, Jesus may come to you. If you love nature and animals, then Lao Zi may come to visit you. If you love the moon, then the moon goddess Diana may come to visit you.

In this manner, you may be selected by more than one Shi Fu. Perhaps when you were a child or young adult you felt a strong attraction to a saint. No one encouraged you to speak with that saint directly, yet you still prayed to him or her, and you did not know why you felt this connection. Then as you grew older, another saint carried particular meaning for you. Again, you did not know why. Your logical mind did not understand. Your soul did.

These are but small examples of a saint trying to connect with you. You have a certain feeling and you pray. You start your prayer by calling in that saint. As you open spiritually, you will hear the saint answering you. You may be able to carry on a conversation with the saint. This is how the saint selects you. This is one means to becoming your Shi Fu.

There will be more than one Shi Fu as you progress in your spiritual journey. Pay homage to them each day, each hour, each minute. Receive their blessings and guidance and always thank them as they enter into you.

In this manner, you will be living in divine relationship with your Shi Fu.

The Third Most Important
Divine Relationship is with Your Teacher

Finding Your Teacher

You are very fortunate if you find your teacher. With his or her guidance, you can more quickly reach the top soul levels. Your teacher is a direct channel to God. You are also a direct channel to God. My task as your teacher is to make your channel more powerful, to make it more accurate, to lead you to the door of soul enlightenment. This is the first day in this new beginning for the journey of your soul.

This is why you need me as your teacher. "Obedience" means to listen to the guidance that comes from God through me. "Obedience" means to follow the guidance of God. This is honoring God.

You must also be devoted. "Devotion" is to fully give your heart. "Devotion" is to kiss the feet of God. "Devotion" is to be a humble servant. If you wish me to be your teacher, you must place devotion as the second most important quality in a disciple.

Lastly, as a humble student, you must show gratitude before you can become my disciple. "Gratitude" is to be in a state of humility, awe and thankfulness each moment.

You may think that it is you who finds your teacher. Only on the outside does this appear to be true. Look deeper for the true meaning here.

You must pass the teacher's test before you are allowed to enter. This teacher's test is to examine your very soul to see if you are obedient to God, devoted to God, and have gratitude to God. If you demonstrate these qualities, then you may be considered for becoming a student.

What I have just told you is all happening in the Soul World. In the Soul World, things move quickly and happen earlier than on the Earth plane and in the physical world.

So once a teacher finds that you are qualified to apply to become a student, then you, in the physical world, have a thought that could lead you to stand in front of your teacher. You may think you somehow arranged this meeting. You may think it is you who have found him. In fact, God and your past karma have brought you to this point at this moment. The meeting between your teacher and you was preordained and arranged in the Soul World.

In fact, it is your teacher who has found and then tested you. This testing started before you had the thought to find this teacher. What I am saying is that sometimes your logical head is the last part of you to be informed as to what your soul is really planning.

As I have told you before, many of you have been my students and even my disciples in past lives. We have a big job to do together. That is why you are meeting me now through my words in this book. This book is part of my divine relationship with you.

You may in your lifetime have several teachers, some before me and some after me. That is fine. I have had several teachers also. All true teachers follow the order of finding students in the manner I have just described. A serious master creates a high-level disciple. If you wish to realize the purpose of your soul's journey in a single lifetime, you must become a serious student and work very hard. When a teacher taps you to come, do not hesitate for a moment to take the opportunity.

How do you recognize your teacher? Your teacher will touch your heart. Your body will shake. Your tears will flow like water. You will hear with your heart the truth as he or she speaks. You will drink deeply, as these words are food for your soul.

You have been waiting for a long time to meet your teacher. It could be that you are being selected even now by your teacher as you read these words. I am speaking directly to your soul.

Honoring Your Teacher

How do you honor your teacher? This is a very important question. I have learned that in the West many people do not know what it truly means. They do not understand the depth of this divine relationship. I will speak with you in great detail about honoring your teacher. Your teacher is one of the golden keys to your full enlightenment.

Appreciation

To show appreciation is to honor your teacher.

- Appreciation is to say, "Thank you so very much. Thank you for helping me find my way in this precious life. I could not have done it without your guidance."

- Appreciation has a quality of gratitude that leads us to feel cared for and thankful. It is often when we are struggling and feeling that life is difficult that we so very much appreciate a helping hand. When we get lost, we appreciate the thoughtfulness and kindness coming from another. We appreciate it most when we are hurting. We are then like little children seeking help from our mother or father.

- Appreciating your teacher is having the mental clarity to recognize that without the level of blessing you receive through your teacher, you could not have grown as fast as you have. Your teacher opens the door for you to the entire Soul World. Your teacher opens the door for you to ancient secret wisdom. Your teacher quickly guides you to the best results in the development of your soul.

- Appreciating your teacher means that you acknowledge on the deepest possible level the invaluable service that your teacher provides. Appreciation lives in your heart.

- Appreciation can also be spoken out loud. Words can be shared with others or with your teacher about what you are learning and how it is changing your life. Share your appreciation, for it may inspire others to learn and change their lives.

- Appreciation of your teacher's guidance and blessing continues on even after you have parted company with your teacher on the physical plane.

- There are even disciples who surpass the level of their teacher. Even these most extraordinary disciples will always first show appreciation to their teacher. Part of being a top-level disciple is that you always honor your teacher.

This ability to honor your teacher and the cultivation of compassion are two of the highest qualities a true disciple must demonstrate.

Respect

Honoring is shown through respect. Respect has many qualities: to admire, to leave as is, to treat as sacred, and to bow down to. Each of these traits is an aspect of respect.

To Admire

Respect implies that you look up to and admire your teacher because you recognize your teacher as a being on a higher level of development than you are at this time.

By having someone in a physical body, a human being like yourself, but one who can demonstrate the abilities, the powers, the capabilities and the consciousness, and who has the wisdom of the Soul World, you can better relate to your teacher. I am in a human body for this reason. If I were pure light, you could not relate to me as easily. Nor could I guide you as well.

Yet your soul can see deeper than my human form, and it is my soul that you are admiring. It is your human nature that needs to see me in human form. Your soul does not. Your soul can understand beyond the human form. That is why you cry when you hear my words: they have no form, yet they deeply touch your soul.

To Leave As Is

Showing respect also means "to leave as is." What is the meaning here? You may have expectations about your teacher, a picture of how he or she is to treat you. This is your human mind or your ego trying to be the boss. Your ego is coming from a small, very small, perspective on the entire universe. So to open your mind, you must also let go of your ego's expectations about how I teach you. That is my job, not yours!

I find that people in the West are always wanting me to teach the way they think a teacher must teach. And yet, they do not understand the deep spiritual principles that guide a teacher. They may want me to run my business according to their prior business experience in the physical world. That is good. I respect them. Yet this is a spiritual teacher teaching from the spiritual world. In the spiritual world, we have our own ways of doing business to help our teachings go out to the public.

So part of respect is for students to open their minds and allow me, as their teacher, to show them new ways. This is how they will grow and leave behind their old beliefs and ways of seeing the physical world.

Another meaning of "leave as is" is to honor your teacher in the words that you speak about him or her. Whether you speak bad words out loud or criticize your teacher in your mind, it makes no difference. I call this "funny thinking." Thinking bad thoughts about your teacher is recorded in the Soul World. It is an example of poor behavior as a student. This kind of thinking is negative and will negatively affect the cultivation of your own soul. This is very deep. It touches upon the quality of purity of your soul.

If I make a mistake, I will quickly see my error and apologize. I too must be pure and set a good example. That is my business. Your business is to purify your own soul.

To Treat As Sacred

To treat as sacred is such a very special quality of honoring your teacher. Think for a moment: who really is it that you are treating as sacred? If you perceive the sacred in me, who is doing the perceiving? Why, of course, it is you who are perceiving! By recognizing the sacred in me, you are also honoring the sacred in you.

Throughout this small book on living divine relationships, I have already shown you an alignment with the universe that is essential to your soul's successful journey in this lifetime. This alignment is first with God, next with your Shi Fu, and then next with your teacher.

This alignment is between your soul and God, your Shi Fu, and your teacher. This aspect of honoring your teacher is to help you cultivate this proper alignment, which is most important. It is, therefore, your soul that is treating these relationships as sacred. This is the proper attitude, the attitude that will open the door for you.

Let us now jump to the next level of meaning of "to treat as sacred." As you open, you will use your Third Eye and your heart to see me and hear me in a new way. You will receive transmissions that come from the Creator directly. As these moments of divine connection happen, you will directly perceive the Divine within me. You may see light of many colors. You may hear both song and silence and words within your heart. You will go to the heart of God.

This is most sacred. I have deep faith that you understand the significance of what I have just said to you. This is why you treat your teacher in a manner that is sacred. This goes far deeper than doing things like putting candles upon an altar. Such practices are good also, but the real point here is the direct connection with the Divine.

"To treat as sacred" comes in many forms. I will tell you but a few. If you can, ask me to directly bless my book for you. When I do this, I place a divine blessing and divine light into the book. I call this to "kai guang." It is a placing of light such that the living spirit of God abides in the book. Then you take this book and place it upon your altar, on the upper right-hand side.

It is also considered showing proper respect to treat as sacred any photograph you have of your teacher. Place this photograph in the center of your altar, somewhat above the other pieces in this shrine.

If you know your Shi Fu or your teacher's teacher, place his or her photograph or image slightly above mine or that of your teacher. This is a demonstration of the proper alignment I have spoken of already.

"To treat as sacred" also means that any writing or paper that you have collected from your teacher never be placed upon the floor. This would be disrespectful. Always place spiritual teachings above the ground and above the level of your waist.

When you sit and listen to your teacher, never point the bottoms of your feet towards your master. This shows disrespect.

When your teacher is walking with you, always allow your teacher to go first. Be courteous and open the door and let your teacher pass first.

When you are eating with your teacher, always wait for your teacher to take the first bite. Even if you are doing silent prayers, and even if your teacher is doing silent prayers before eating, still wait for your teacher to eat first.

When your teacher asks you to do something, treat this request as sacred. It may carry more meaning than the mere task or mere words involved. Remember, the spiritual world records your thoughts. Being asked to do something has many levels of significance within it. The first is to say "yes" to the sacred. The second is to learn how to obey the wishes of God. I will speak more about this later.

The last is a most important point. As you demonstrate to the spiritual world, and as you demonstrate to your teacher that you understand what it means to "treat as sacred," God will reveal himself

to you with greater frequency. This is such a blessing! This is deep
spiritual wisdom.

To Bow Down To

To "bow down" to has deep meaning. The humility, the lack of
ego, the recognition of another soul, the recognition of the divinity in
all souls, the total and pure devotion to God, your Shi Fu and your
teacher, the depth of commitment to this devotion in this lifetime,
the direct demonstration of appreciation and respect, all of these are
present in the act of bowing down.

- To bow down can be done first thing every day when you get
  out of bed.

- To bow down can be done when you see your teacher.

- To bow down can be done when you see any teacher you
  respect.

- To bow down is part of daily prostrations, be they full-body to
  the floor or merely touching your head to the ground.

- To bow down is to reflect back to the soul in front of you that
  you receive and perceive the divinity of that soul.

- To bow down is to give direct thanks to God for a blessing, for
  a prayer, for an inspiration, for a thought that has come to you.
  Always give thanks to God in these moments.

- To bow down is to directly give thanks to your teacher for any
  transmission, blessing, task, words or actions that your teacher
  has conveyed to you or given to you as a gift.

- To bow down is the first and the last appropriate action to take when greeting and leaving your teacher's presence. This type of bowing down may be only a tilt of your head downward, or bending your body at the waist, or placing your knees to the floor and touching your head to the ground, or laying your full body on the ground with your hands in the prayer position in front of your head. This is known as supplication. This is a sacred gesture.

- To bow down is also done not just with the physical body. To speak the words, "I bow down .... I honor you," is most important in your prayers and requests for blessings of the soul, mind, and body.

- To bow down is to be done as recognition of the role of your teacher, and of your teacher's teacher, and of your teacher's many Shi Fus, and of the total lineage of enlightened beings who have preceded you. You bow down to the entire lineage. You may do this as part of your prayers or you may do this in thought and word.

- To bow down when you write a book is to place a photograph of your teacher in front of any words about yourself. This is the proper alignment and giving of thanks and gratitude for the many blessings you have received.

- To bow down when you receive the results of a blessing you have asked for is to give full recognition of the gift you have been given by your teacher and his virtue or merit.

Do a Good Job!

In addition to showing appreciation and respect, there is another way to honor your teacher. Do a good job! Take all my teachings, take all my blessings, take all my transmissions, pass all my tests, transform your life and do a good job at it! Make me proud of you! Show me how you have taken all the efforts that I pour into you, show me how much you have learned!

For my heart, as your teacher, is moved when I see you grow. You feed my soul the most, not when you say nice words to me or speak to others in an admiring tone …. you feed my soul the most when you offer service, unconditionally, and serve God, unconditionally.

This is honoring me. For I honor God in this manner. You give praise to me, and I, as your teacher, give it all back to God.

That's it! That is the only way to do it!

Honor me in your heart. Honor me as you pray to God. Honor me as you help others.

In conclusion to this special section that holds a golden key for your soul's journey, I wish to add a few final words that I hope you will always remember. Everything I have said to you about how to honor your teacher will bring more light into you. This will transform you! I am showing you the proper path, the proper behavior, the proper actions, the proper thinking to bring you to the door of your own enlightenment.

It is only when you learn to do all of this that the vessel of your soul, mind and body will be cleansed and prepared for the ultimate divine relationship. As you learn how to do all that I have told you, you will begin each day living in divine relationship. This will transform your life.

Three Keys to Spiritual Growth

Three simple words that you must always remember are the spiritual keys to the successful journey of your soul in this lifetime: G. O. D. Yes, you are reading the word God. To spiritually grow, you must always remember God. But pay close attention because here the word "God" has periods after each letter. This means it is a secret formula.

What is the secret here? "G" stands for gratitude. "O" stands for obedience. "D" stands for devotion. These three qualities must be cultivated within you as the student.

Gratitude, obedience and devotion to whom? To God. When I speak of gratitude, I mean total gratitude to God.

Total Gratitude to God

"Gratitude" means you acknowledge the state of divine grace. When you feel grateful, you are in the state of divine grace. What I am saying here is that you enter a state of divine grace, and in that state, what you are feeling is so very grateful for all that is given to you – your life, your children, your opportunity to be of service to others, your opportunity to hear precious spiritual teachings. These are only some of the reasons you feel grateful. You feel blessed in your life. And knowing how very special these blessings are, you feel grateful to God.

Gratitude is a most special emotion. Gratitude has a sweetness and a softness as it surrounds you and comes into your heart. Gratitude is so soft. It holds you tenderly. Tears may well up in your eyes. You may stop for a moment to gaze upon a flower or look more deeply into the sky. You feel touched. You feel connected to God.

Within this softness, this quality of love, there arises inside you a deep wave of appreciation of the many gifts placed before you. This is the wave of divine grace that builds inside you. As you feel it coming, you may bow down to say, "Thank you, dear God, for I understand more and more."

In these moments when you directly feel this profound appreciation, you are in the divine grace of God, and you are being blessed. You are living in divine relationship with God.

So far, I have told you what you receive in this state of gratitude. But it goes deeper than just you. You must also forget about yourself to truly grow spiritually.

It is about God. This is the focus. Gratitude is expressed to God. God receives our thanks, our appreciation, our love, and our respect. God hears and sees and knows what lives within our hearts. There are no secrets. God knows our deepest feelings.

To express total gratitude to God is food for God's soul. God has done such a remarkable job, such an act of divine creation, each moment, for thousands of eons. Now it is time for us, for you and for me, to give thanks in return. Our thanks may be small compared to the total picture of divine creation, yet our thanks count in the heart of God.

God receives your gratitude. And in the act of receiving your gratitude, God gives it back to you as divine grace. That is how it works.

And as a teacher, a spiritual master, I set an example for you. You give thanks to me, you express your gratitude for what I teach you, and immediately I give all the thanks back to God. This is most important: always give it back to God.

As I have taught you earlier in this small book, we live in relationship to others. To live in divine relationship with God is to both give and receive — from God to you and back to God. This connection happens in a cycle that builds strength and will gradually transform your entire life. It will also transform your ability to offer service to God. You will become increasingly a servant of God's will. This is what God receives as you grow spiritually. You are building a home for God in your human heart. You are always in God's heart.

This is how your divine relationship with God can grow.

Yet, there is one more part to this. It is the most pure of all. You express total gratitude to God simply because you see the exquisite truth of his creation. You are in a state of awe. You wake up! You see the perfection, the beauty, the infinite connectedness, and your mind opens to a freedom that is vast. For all of this, you and I are grateful.

This is why we bow down to give thanks. This is how we enter living in divine relationship with God through cultivating the emotion and practice of total gratitude.

Total Obedience to God

Exercising "total obedience" to God is to follow God's will. Now some of you may not know how to find God's will. You may not understand what this means and how to find it. Let me help you.

Up until your reading of this small book, your life may have been directed by your logical mind. Today however, as you read these words, it is not your logical thinking that is being moved. It is your soul. So the first thing that must happen inside you is that your soul needs to become the boss of your life. Once this happens, your soul will have a better chance to connect with the will of God.

Inside your soul is a quality of humility. Humility allows you to let go of the pretense of knowing everything already. Humility allows you to be open and to listen. Humility allows you the patience to see what unfolds in front of you. Humility is supple and flexible. Humility has equanimity, a balance and an accepting of the life lessons in front of you.In the state of humility, we are but babies learning each moment something beyond our ordinary thinking. In the state of humility, we bow down to follow Divine Guidance because we know that we do not know. We seek help from a larger and wiser soul. That is the soul of God.

Through the state of humility, we begin to hear guidance. We begin to see that there is a path being shown to us. We are finding the pathway of God's will. We are finding our divine purpose in this lifetime. We are having a conversation with God. We are finding our daily expression of living God's will. As this unfolds in front of us, we begin to see what we must follow. We begin to know how to find it. This is an attitude that becomes a practice each day for each decision and for each interaction.

"Total obedience to God" means that many times you will not know what you are going to do, or what you are going to say. There is a surrender inside. You must be willing to stand on the edge of the precipice and be in the state of not knowing. This is the giving up of your ego and the opening to the guidance of God. You must come to trust exactly at that point where you are most scared of the unknown. You come to be empty. Now you are a vessel for God's work.

Yes, there is a divine plan, and it may take some time for you to truly be comfortable in your place within that plan. You must learn to "let go and let God." When you struggle, you only get in your own way.

Find God's will by listening with your heart. Be open and humble. Accept what is placed in front of you with gratitude. Say "yes" when you are asked to do something by your teacher who is showing you the way.

In this manner, you enter the pathway of God's will. Be assured that the spiritual unfolding that will come to you, that will speed your spiritual growth, will be quicker as you practice total obedience to God.

Each day, each action, each thought is an opportunity to be living in divine relationship with God, and that relationship is one of

humility and bowing to greater wisdom. Find your place through following God's will.

Total Devotion to God

Once you feel the divine grace of God, you will be humbled.
Then it follows that you will be so touched that you will want, more
than anything in your entire life, to devote yourself to the bliss, the
purity, the very essence of God's heart.

Once you personally and directly experience this, there is no
question about the purpose of your life. Your life purpose is to ful-
fill your spiritual journey to enlightenment, and in this process to
devotedly serve all souls, wherever they may be, in this universe
and beyond.

"Devotion" is to commit to fully follow the path that so touches
your heart. Once you discover this path, there is no stopping your
progress. Friends or family may say you are crazy, but you know
differently. Your values are no longer of the physical world with its
material wealth or power. You are changing onto the spiritual path
where you are finding a relationship between yourself and the infinite
universe of many souls.

Remember to stay humble. Your path may not be the path for a
friend. That is fine. Never force your path upon another. Each soul
must find his or her own way. This is part of God's divine plan. To see
this wisdom, you need only look upon the difference in people's faces.
God made each of us different and unique. We each have our own
lessons to complete. Always be respectful of these differences. Love

the uniqueness of each soul. By allowing for these differences, you are also seeing the many manifestations of God's subdivided soul.

God has created differences and similarities. To all of this divine creation be forever appreciative, grateful, humble, respectful and devoted.

The feeling of devotion is most sacred and honoring. Bring this quality into your daily life. As you look into the eyes of another, know that you are directly relating to a subdivided soul of God. Treat this person in front of you as you would God. This is living in divine relationship with God through expressing total devotion. This is the deeper meaning of placing our hands in the prayer position and bowing down to another, be that person a lover, a friend, or your teacher.

God is a living presence in each moment and in each form and beyond. See this and know this. Practice and live by these three golden keys of total gratitude, total obedience and total devotion. Your journey will open!

Past Lives with Your Teacher

Part of understanding how we fit into the universe and God's creation is to hold the possibility in our minds that our soul has lived many lifetimes. For some, I realize, this is only an abstract idea. For others, it is a living truth.

As your spiritual channels open, and as your ego lets go of trying to be the boss, you will catch glimpses of times gone by, times before this lifetime. You both were and were not yourself. Your ego was not present. By this, I mean your personality. Yet your soul was. Perhaps you can understand it in this way, as a part of you journeys through time.

During these journeys you have lived in many forms, including stones, rivers, animals, plants and now as a human. It is very rare to enter into the human form. It is most precious because it is the best time to learn spiritual teachings that will help you realize enlightenment.

"Enlightenment" is the opportunity to enter the gate into the many realms of Heaven. It is the opportunity to return to the source of God's heart. This is home.

We fall from our home into many physical lifetimes. We can also have lifetimes where we have no form and live in the spiritual realms. We can be good and we can be dark. There is no judgment here. It is our karma that attracts us into these various lifetimes.

What am I saying here? I am giving you deep spiritual wisdom. Being in the human form that you are today is to be taken as a most precious time. Make great progress during this lifetime! Practice hard what I am teaching you.

Now that you have heard some of the meaning of living many lifetimes, and now that you have learned how very special is this lifetime, we must go deeper.

There is a divine plan. You are part of it. You can accept the opportunity given to you or not. It is your choice. Choose wisely.

If you choose to be alienated and filled with despair, your life will reflect that. If you choose to realign your soul with God, your life will reflect that too.

Part of loving yourself enough to see your connection with God and with those around you is to open, open, open to everything. See the beauty and the wonder and the perfection! This is seeing with your physical eyes.

Then go deeper and see with your internal vision, see the formless universe of souls and saints around you. Then you will see me differently. You will see me as your teacher, as a manifestation of Jesus, Mary, Allah, Buddha, Light. Whatever you perceive reflects how open your spiritual channels are.

Perceive beyond this physical lifetime. How have we related before? Have I been part of your life before? What was our relationship? Why are you drawn to the teachers you have met in this lifetime?

Your special relationship with your spiritual teacher is most precious. It is a book that has many chapters. Perhaps you have been brother and sister. Perhaps you have been mother and child. Perhaps you have been a general and killed your enemy. Perhaps you have been lovers.

Each of the many possibilities has brought both thoughts and actions that have good and not-so-good karma. Where the story ended in a prior lifetime together, the next lifetime will continue from that point. This means that each lifetime brings the opportunity to completely, totally, clear and clean whatever loose ends exist between you and your teacher.

I will give you a true story. Two lifetimes ago, I was spiritual master to a most devoted student. I gave him a task. He never completed this task. Now, in this lifetime, I meet him again. Again, I give him the same task. He struggles so hard to complete this task. Why? Because there is greater testing, greater resistance that has accumulated through these two lifetimes. If it was difficult the first time, it now is more than two times more difficult.

He is a good student. He can overcome many struggles. But this particular one has been impossible for him to master. The reason is simple: it contains the difficulty of more than one lifetime. It is also so very important. When he does complete this task, he will be clear for all future lifetimes. This is how great the impact is for the journey of his soul.

As a spiritual master, I too must set a good example. If you have hurt me or harmed me in any way, I forgive you. I practice total forgiveness. God has given me many tests and tasks. These are each opportunities to "let go and let God." This means to totally obey the path that God places in front of me. I too, like you, have many lessons to learn. I must welcome God's plan, receive each lesson, and learn it well in this lifetime. If I do not, then I must repeat it again in the future.

So far I have spoken about your discovering our past lives together. I also have access to that information. The truth is that a spiritual master can look into the Akashic Records and quickly see your past lives as well as your future lives. So when I accept you as a student, I have already seen you.

Have you ever in your life experienced being totally seen into and totally loved? How deeply our souls yearn for this unconditional love. That is what I offer you — my unconditional love.

As I extend my hand to yours, accept me, walk with me on this journey. In this manner, we will live in divine relationship in this lifetime. We will complete, cleanse, heal, accept, and move into the true freedom that our souls long for so deeply. Now we are ready for divine service. Notice that I say "we." I bring you to this door. You must walk through it. This is part of our relationship. This is my job. Now you must do yours.

The Soul of Your Teacher

See me as a wise human being, and I will be that for you.

See me as a spiritual master, and I will be that for you.

See me a divine light and Buddha nature, and I will be that for you.

See me as God's heart and soul, and I will be that for you.

I will be for you as you allow me to be. Again, this is your choice, your karma, your openness, your willingness to trust, your ability to enter into spaces that are new and unknown to your logical mind. Your discipline, your steadfastness, your commitment give you the strength to perceive me more clearly as time goes by.

Remember, you may perceive my soul only ten per cent, but I perceive your soul one hundred per cent. That is why I am the teacher and you are the student. In time, you too may be the teacher. Our job is a big job, and we need many open, enlightened teachers.

What am I saying here? First, you may not be allowed to see my soul unless I open to you. And even when I open to you, you perceive only a small part. Why? Because you are still opening your spiritual channels.

Let me help you to understand. My soul is most ancient. Many is the time I have sat in the heavens next to God, and many is the time I have come to this planet Earth to be of service. My soul works very hard to gain the virtue necessary to do a big job for the entire universe. This job will take place over many lifetimes. Some are in the past, and some are in the future.

My soul is a servant, vehicle and channel. I am of the Light.

I bring together all sides, the light and the dark, and help them to realize soul enlightenment. It is my duty to be of universal service bringing all souls in this universe and beyond into soul enlightenment.

This is the Era of the Soul Light. Many of us have been together before to prepare for this very era, and it will last for thousands of years. I share this with you because your soul wants to know and wants to help.

As a servant and vehicle, I have entered into many souls of saints that you may recognize. This is because my soul is coming directly from the heart of God, as a son of God, a vehicle and channel of infinite light and love.

My soul has the ability to heal and bless, removing obstacles from your past. My soul can give you great gifts of power, compassion, and the ability to enlighten others.

My soul is a river of God's golden, liquid light.

I bless you from the bottom of my heart. May each of you live in divine relationship with God.

4

Sacred Hierarchies

Soul Level

What I am about to teach you now is wisdom that few spiritual masters will openly share. For many centuries, spiritual masters have kept such high-level secrets to themselves. They do not openly tell their students, even close students, these secrets. I believe it is time, as the Soul Light Era begins, to openly tell you these closely held secrets.

The first secret is that your precious soul comes into this life with a special level assigned to it at birth. By "level," I mean the soul is given a number that reflects its purity and its wisdom. Many people recognize when a baby is born that it has a soul. It is common for people to say, "This is an old soul." Or they will say the opposite, "This is a new soul." So people in general do understand old and new souls.

What is not understood is that there are many steps, or what I call "levels" between old and new. There are actually 108 levels that reflect the development of a soul.

ery soul has God's subdivided soul within it. In this manner, of you can express the Divine and know the nature of God's heart. This potential can grow much greater than it is for you today. It is important that you understand that the seed is already planted inside you. For many, however, that seed, that potential, is only partially spiritually awake.

Wake up! That is my message to you. Wake up! Let your soul come out! The more you connect with your soul, the more your soul can really progress on its journey. In this precious lifetime, you have the opportunity to wake up your soul to its true potential!

Do you understand what I am saying here? This is an idea much bigger than your logical thinking can understand. I am speaking directly to your soul. Listen carefully: you were born with your soul at a certain level. You have the opportunity to develop your soul further if you will do what I am teaching here. You have the opportunity to bring your soul to the level of soul enlightenment in this single lifetime!

At this time, the level of your soul is set by your past karma and your many past lifetimes. In the Akashic Records, the spiritual book that records all deeds and thoughts, there is the complete story of your many lifetimes. Remember that in the spiritual world, there are no secrets! In the Akashic book, your spiritual merits are weighed between your good deeds and your not-so-good deeds. I call this your "karmic record." One side is weighed against the other for any particular life. At the end of that life, the balance scale tells Heaven's Team where your soul level is. Then, as you get ready to be born again, your soul level is assigned to you. This is the soul level you come into this lifetime with at birth.

While it is your soul that brings you to read this book and study these teachings, you still are blocked from your full potential of soul enlightenment. You must work very hard and overcome many obstacles to develop your soul and go higher. Think of it this way: visualize stairs and see your soul stepping from one step to a higher step until you get to the top. This is the doorway to soul enlightenment. Then, of course, there is a new set of stairs. These new stairs represent an even higher level of cultivation of the soul. These stairs are for mind enlightenment and body enlightenment.

This is the true purpose of your soul journey in this lifetime. As you come to truly, deeply bring these teachings into your heart, you will feel blessed, for your journey now has clarity and purpose. You are beginning to wake up. The road in front of you is now clearer in your mind. Your soul feels excitement. You are coming home.

In this manner, you are now beginning to live in divine relationship with your very own soul. How exciting! How wonderful! How blessed!

Soul World Hierarchy

"As above, so below." What is the meaning here? Just as you know of the physical world with its rules and regulations, know also that there is a similar code in the spiritual world.

In the physical world, you accept and even live each day with complete comfort and agreement that there are laws: laws for driving your car, protocols for polite behavior, a president to your country, etc. You live within a social structure that reflects power and prestige. You acknowledge the abilities of people in these positions. You respect them and you obey them. That is how we all exist together. When we do not agree, that is when wars begin.

I remind you of that which may seem obvious because I want your mind to picture the same social structures existing in the spiritual realm. In the spiritual realm, it is even more serious because the powers and abilities are greater. The importance of spiritual recognition of the level of one's soul is key to the entire social code within the spiritual realm. What is the meaning here?

Because the souls in the spiritual realm are already enlightened, they are very familiar with what must be done to realize these highest states of cultivation. They spent many lifetimes to realize their own levels of enlightenment. They know what it is to practice. They understand respect and obedience. They know how to purify their minds. They understand service. They have themselves dedicated countless lifetimes to be able to enter the various heavenly realms and be seated amongst the saints and holy masters. Because of their diligent work, they deeply understand the importance of recognizing the level of each soul in the heavenly realms. You could accurately say they are well trained.

There is a wheel of life that has within it many different realms. There are more realms than just Heaven and Hell. There are more realms than just the spiritual and the physical. There exist in Heaven many different realms. These realms are like kingdoms. There are heads of each realm with accompanying saints, bodhisattvas, healing masters, spiritual teachers, buddhas, disciples of many spiritual traditions. There are realms of souls who are not enlightened such as the animal realm. There are realms for "hungry ghosts" or souls who are lost and in limbo. There are realms for the dark energies and those stuck in Hell. The human realm is also one of these many realities in the wheel of life.

So a soul that is stuck in the realm of Hell is there because of the negative karmic acts and thoughts he or she has had in this lifetime or in past lifetimes. The level of that soul is very, very low at this time.

A soul in the animal realm is also quite low. Yet an animal may be blessed because you are its owner and you chant each day. Your animal may hear the chanting and recall it as it prepares to die. In this manner, your pet may also attain a higher soul level. It may even be enlightened if, in the moment of death, it thinks of you and your chanting.

A soul of darkness, a soul you may think of as mean and nasty, is also doing its job. Even these souls have a purpose. The level of this soul is quite low because its acts are destructive. This kind of soul may even attach itself to you because it likes your light and is drawn to the light just as we humans are. In the same manner, this kind of dark soul will be drawn to you when you are angry or having a fight with someone. The level of this soul is also quite low.

Within the human realm there are many soul levels possible. Your soul level can also change. I will teach you much more about this in a moment.

To sit in Heaven's realm, your soul must be quite evolved and highly cultivated in its practices. As an enlightened soul in the heavenly realm, you have realized purity and integrity within your mind. You have realized a complete clearing of any negative karma. Your vessel is filled with light. Your heart has boundless compassion. You enter the enlightened state and maintain the enlightened state without ever faltering in your purity and concern for others. You truly are a divine being.

You are given a job to do within this heavenly realm. It is a big job that covers the entire universe and beyond into boundless galaxies. You must always be awake and on duty. There may be countless wandering and lost souls who seek your guidance and your service within each and every moment in time.

With this divine presence, you govern certain areas of the heavenly realm. This is your kingdom. It has its own name. Between these numerous kingdoms there can be strife and discord. The spiritual world is not always peaceful and even that is an understatement.

The point I am making here is that key to all of this very high level of realization is the respect and recognition of the hierarchy of souls. An enlightened soul can totally see the level of another enlightened soul. There are many sub-levels even within the enlightened state. The ability to see with inner vision and the ability to speak to the soul directly enables enlightened souls to know and to see everything. It is also necessary for the soul that is being read in this manner to open fully and reveal itself. High-level souls do not so easily give this access to another. There must be permission given.

The higher the level of the soul, the greater is the power of that soul to do the job. This means the greater is the impact of a blessing, a healing, a thought that leads to manifestation. A soul may exist in the heavenly realm and sit at the feet of another soul. This demonstrates the understanding of soul hierarchy. The soul who sits at a lower level is there because its soul power is known to be less than that of the soul who sits at a higher level.

Now I will tell you a true story that has been witnessed by my close students and disciples. Over the past few years, I have been given many gifts from God directly. These gifts are abilities that enable me to be of better service to others throughout the entire universe and beyond. This is part of my job in the physical form. Yet I come to this job in this physical body because of my countless years, thousands of years throughout many lifetimes, of diligent service and total commitment to God.

A few years ago, I opened my Message Center, my heart chakra, to my students and close disciples to show them and allow them access to the spiritual realm that exists inside my heart. At that time, my presence was only beginning to be recognized in the spiritual realm, yet many of the saints and holy people came when I asked them to gather for a conference.

At that time, they came with some doubt or question as to who this soul was who dared to summon them to a most important conference. As time went by, these very saints and enlightened healers and spiritual teachers would all bring their own disciples who usually sit at their feet. The enlightened souls in the heavens now began to quickly come, to rush in to the circle of our conference.

These saints and enlightened masters heard my worlds and saw my heart and my purity. They began to let their differences wash away and to come together with a more united purpose. They all understand this special and difficult passage of time we are going through. They all understand it is the time, the age of a new spiritual beginning throughout the entire universe and all galaxies. So at these conferences we came to be known as the Spiritual United Nations. My task is to call these souls in and then speak to all of them as they sit in this large circle in my heart.

This has taken many years. Now they listen and they are excited. They all want to work together and get along. But this is not an easy job for me. I know more deeply than you how very difficult it is to bring together souls of such different levels. There can be competition and attachment to their own kingdoms and their own powers. I must be the peacemaker, the negotiator and the true divine servant, vehicle and channel. I will be tested by all of these souls until they fully trust me. This is a big job.

I share this with you now because you must understand the hierarchy of souls that exists on all levels in both the spiritual and physical realms. I am part of that hierarchy and you are part of that hierarchy. I know many of you are Americans and raised in a country that teaches equality. This is not an easy message for you to hear. But listen well: there is a hierarchy of souls. It is very important for the journey of your soul to honor and respect your place and position within that hierarchy. Be humble. Be patient. Be respectful.

As you come to be able to see and to read the soul level of others, you will more deeply know the truth of my words. To be in proper alignment with the Divine, as I have previously taught you, begins with knowing that your first divine relationship is with God. Your next divine relationship is with your Shi Fu or Shi Fus. Your third divine relationship is with your teacher. Your fourth divine relationship is with your soul in relationship to all souls in the universe. Find your place. In this manner you will be living divine relationships while in your physical body.

Raising Your Soul Level

Find your place amongst all souls. Be not attached to this place. Allow my blessings to assist and uplift you. My service is to guide you and to prepare your soul to enter fully into the light. Each blessing I give you helps to clear your negative karma and to bring beautiful light where there has been darkness. These are my gifts to you.

I am bathing you with the golden liquid of the Divine. I hold you lovingly and gently. I wash you and heal you. Your soul shines. This is food for your soul. This helps your soul become strong and pure. This helps your soul become the light. These are my gifts to you. This is my love to you.

As you receive my light and my love, I ask this of you. Give it to another. Whatever gifts I give to you, give to another. Receive my blessings and pass them on to another. Become a funnel from the Divine through me to you and to another. In this manner, you are living in divine relationship with many souls each and every day.

Your soul will grow and grow as you give to another. Yet remember to give purely and freely. Give not to gain for your own soul. Yes, your soul will grow, yet your motivation must be pure. Think of others. You will see that when you do that, your life transforms. As your life transforms, your soul is also changing. These go together and reflect one another.

Your job is to raise your soul level, step by step, during this lifetime. When I ask you what the purpose is of this lifetime for yourself, what do you think is the answer? There is only one answer! Let me be very clear so that you hold this thought in your heart and never forget it.

The purpose of your lifetime is to further the journey of your soul. This means that each obstacle in your life must be seen as a lesson to be learned. Each person who irritates you must be accepted for whom that person is. In any way you hold a mean thought of another, forgive that person and ask that he or she forgive you. Be kind. Think of others. These are but a few of the many ways you can further the journey of your soul. These are small acts you can do each day while you are in the human body.

When you do these small acts, then you can do the bigger tasks. For you to be a golden funnel of God's love, you must be pure and clean. To truly be of service to others, you must yourself be able to pass on divine love and divine light.

And while you are young at this, while your funnel is not yet fully prepared, you still can do many acts for others. Enter into prayer on behalf of other souls before you fully wake up and get out of bed. Bow down to God and Heaven's Team after you get up. Ask to be of good service. Offer prayers to all souls before each meal. Change your thinking from complaints and blaming others to thoughts of kindness and gratitude. Leave behind the "me, me, me" and move into "universal service for all souls."

What I am saying to you here is that no matter who you are or what may be your external circumstances, you can still do what I am telling you. It is so very important because it will help to change and transform our entire world, our universe and galaxy. It is so very important because it will help to transform your very own soul.

You are but a tiny pebble in the great pond of this universe. Yet, as you drop into the pond and make even the tiniest movement, the entire universe changes. Think of this carefully and look deeply into my meaning here. On the one hand, I am saying the level of your soul is that of a baby compared to that of the enlightened masters in the heavenly realms. And yet, on the other hand, I am saying your tiny soul creates ripples in the entire universe. You are both.

If you want to be of true service, if you want to make a difference in this world in this time of chaos and struggle, make a tiny shift in yourself. Do this first. Do this by bowing down to God and telling God directly how grateful you are for this human life. Bow down to all souls. From your heart, ask for peace, wisdom and kindness to exist for all souls in all directions and in all realms. Let your heart and your mind open to serve all souls' light in this manner, for it will help them on their journeys. This is deep service.

This deep and quiet service that I share with you is called "yin" service. There is no plaque on a wall or any announcement of good deeds done. Rather, this service is quiet. It holds greater purity and that is why we call it yin service. It brings great rewards that we call virtue.

There exists in the Soul World a Heaven's Bank. Just as you have a bank in the physical world, there is a bank in the spiritual world. The coin of the realm in the physical world is money. The coin of the realm in the spiritual world is virtue. To progress in the spiritual world you must build virtue.

How do you build virtue? By doing all that I am suggesting to you in these last few teachings about praying for others, having positive thinking, balancing your emotions, and thinking of others. In this manner, your yin service will quickly build.

The "yang" service is the outer actions or words or deeds that are more public and seen by others. This, too, is important for different reasons. The primary virtue here is gained because you are sharing with others. For those souls who need to live more in the physical world, and need to hear the teachings in the physical world, for them you must share in a physical manner. You can do this in many ways. You can write books or articles. You can speak directly to another.

You can teach. You can offer money for good causes like food and shelter for the poor.

Yet the most important quality to share is what I call "soul food." It is sharing with your words how you are touched in your heart when you connect with the Divine. It is sharing with your words how deeply my teachings have helped you to transform your life. It is sharing your own personal and direct experiences that bring tears to your eyes. People who hear these words will feel the ripple in their hearts. In this manner you are causing transformation to begin within them. This is the deepest service. You are helping other souls to find their way.

Connecting with many souls is living in divine relationship. By living each day and each hour in this manner, you will also change the level of your own soul. Your soul will evolve and move up the stairs that I described to you. Remember, this stairway exists only while you are in this human form. That is why this human life is so very precious.

Purity of Your Soul

"Purity of the soul" is a condition we each must wish to achieve. What is the meaning here? Because purity will open the door to Heaven and take you directly to God's heart, purity is a key, one of the more important key qualities we each must cultivate.

To live in God's heart brings joy to you and to those around you. You radiate pure joy! People can see your joy. They can see the special quality of purity that radiates from your face and from deep within your eyes.

To live in God's heart will transform your entire soul journey. To live in God's heart will transform every aspect of your daily life. To live in God's heart will place you in a position of great and everlasting service to other souls. You will be an example. You will have a big job in front of you. Purity is the key to this journey of your soul. To live in a state of purity your soul will have already reached a very high level.

- Purity is to become so clear that you are a crystalline diamond reflecting all colors in the entire universe. There is not a single speck of dust. All is pristine, light, exquisite beyond your ordinary thinking.

- Purity radiates the highest vibration of light and sound waves into the entire universe.

- Purity is brilliant like a thousand suns.

- Purity carries the gentleness of divine love.

- Purity listens and hears the voice of God giving utmost obedience to the divine word.

- Purity is total devotion to the divine word of God.

- Purity is living inside the channel that God has created to connect with you.

- Purity is living in alignment with God and in accordance with his guidance.

• Purity is living inside the heart of God and God living inside your heart.

This is living in divine relationship. Your soul is pure, clear, brilliant, hearing Divine Guidance as you move through each day and minute. This is the seamless condition of your life with God while in the physical body. It is so very important to know that the Divine is living inside your heart.

As your soul level goes higher, you will more deeply understand what it means that the Divine is living inside your heart. You will understand that "sacred hierarchies" are sacred and made of the Divine. You will find your place and position in these sacred hierarchies. Your position is at one place now as you read my words. Your position can change as a result of reading my words. Your position can go higher and higher as you apply the teachings I give you within these words. This means that within this precious lifetime, you can achieve a pure soul that is living in divine relationship with God.

What greater gift can I give you than for you to receive this wisdom? This wisdom will give you hope, will give you inspiration that within your lifetime you can live within the heart of God.

Some of my close disciples have come with me into the heart of God. They know the truth of my words. They come only for a short time, for a blessing and for a transmission of my special gifts to them. Think now of this: a short time will come and will go. A short time will totally transform your life. Now, think of this: to live in the heart of God is forever. This means all the time, ever present in the heart of God, in this life and in all your future lives. This is beyond your ordinary thinking!

I give to you my first golden key: purify your soul!

Soul Abilities

In the very beginning, before time and space, before light or dark, out of the immeasurable and boundless emptiness came a movement, a fluid ripple and growing wave that filled all the vastness. As this wave rose, all of the emptiness also moved. Then the emptiness opened further and from within its center, behind its outer reaches, came an energy of great power. This force moved so quickly through the formless emptiness that shock waves arose.

Waves of movement went in all directions where before there were no directions. As they fell upon themselves, the impact was so great that small particles were forced to adhere to one another. The forces in all directions continued to build and soon to explode. More small particles were created. A vacuum of negative force built up and swallowed the small particles, thus creating the beginning of duality, of form and formless. The first distinctions arose out of this boundless emptiness. This was the universe giving birth to itself.

How do I know this? Because I was there. There was no I. Yet within me in each cell is the wisdom, the knowledge of this birth. This is the Source.

Become very quiet now as you listen to my words. I will take you as far as your soul will allow me. Open yourself. Open yourself and come with me.

Inside each cell in my body is a universe that is in the act of recreating its own destruction and creation. There is a constant death and birth. In the death, there is no form. In the birth, the form begins. Inside my mind, I can go inside any cell and be fully present to the universal forces at work. I need only to focus there and the entire universe will open to me again.

As I rest in this focus, my mind is very still. There is no thought. I go into the emptiness. It is within the emptiness that the great blessings, gifts, wisdom teachings come to me. I can realize this on the cellular level. The Source is within every cell. I know this consciously. I am a total manifestation of the Source. When I go there in my mind, I am returning to the Source. Because the emptiness is beyond time and space, I can enter there and return to the beginning of all creation because all creation is beginning now.

Let your logical thinking go. Continue to come with me. Time is only a dimension. Time is spontaneous. What matters is how far you can go into the emptiness. Then within all your cells you can return to the Source in a moment.

This is rejuvenation. This is mind enlightenment.

Inside the Source is pure light, no light, movement and stillness. All great paradoxes are unified in this state of Oneness out of which creation of the universe arises.

What I teach my students is that the entire universe lives within my heart. That is true. Yet it is only the beginning, the first level of high-level teachings. What I have not taught them is what I am now telling you.

The entire universe is still limited to both a time and space dimension. Go further. Each cell also contains an entire universe. As I receive the highest blessings and gifts from God, these enter into each and every cell within my entire body. Go further. Beyond any concept of God, beyond the entire universe, is the ultimate Source that is present within me, and I am part of it around me. There is a total immersion without distinctions.

How do I know this? I know this because my soul travels to this physical body and comes from the Source. My soul has many abilities. One of those abilities is to return to the Source. Each time I return to the Source, the rejuvenation is so profound that my body increasingly embodies higher frequencies that are more similar to the Source. This changes my DNA and RNA and the smallest particles until I am more perfectly reflecting the Source.

This is body enlightenment.

In both states of mind enlightenment and body enlightenment, my soul has increasingly higher powers or abilities. Soul abilities come as your soul opens. Inside you are many flowers that show your soul level and your soul abilities. When you open, you can see these flowers. They tell your teacher the level of your enlightenment. So you are like a flower that opens to the gifts from God and the entire heavenly realm.

God will continue to give you divine gifts beyond your imagination. God gives me gifts that are beyond your logical thinking. And I give them to you and to my devoted students.

For each soul there are special divine gifts because your soul is special. Your flowers are special and show your unique virtues and soul talents. When God gives his gifts to further your soul development and to bring greater soul abilities, he knows your special soul and he gives in a special way just to you.

I guide you and teach you how to open your soul, how to purify your soul, mind, and body. God then gives to you as you realize each new level. He recognizes you. I am his servant, vehicle and channel. I teach you and I bless you. I cleanse you and prepare you. It is you who must walk through the doorway into these higher levels of soul cultivation.

Your soul will travel through many lifetimes. Your job is to raise the level of your soul as much as possible in each lifetime. In this lifetime is a most special opportunity. You have met me and you are hearing my teachings. We have met before, many times. This time is different because you can raise your soul level to the highest level and at the time of your death, you can enter the heavenly realm and sit with the highest saints, bodhisattvas, and enlightened masters. This is the door that I bring you to and show to you. Be diligent and practice well.

This doorway opens and you will walk through it. In this manner, you will be living in divine relationship in Heaven's kingdom.

Your Soul is the Boss of Your Life

Connect Your Soul to God Daily

My most precious sons and daughters, listen carefully to this simple guidance I give to you now. I have spoken to you already about aligning your soul to God, and next to your Shi Fu or personal guide, and then with your spiritual master. Now, I will tell you how to do this most important daily task.

Connect with God each day. In the very beginning of your spiritual journey, you may think of this perhaps only once or twice. That is good too. However, there is so very much more. The time is so short. Do not let yourself get lazy and think you have done enough. It is not so. There can never be enough done when it comes to being in relationship with the Divine.

Let me be an example for you. I connect with God many times each day. By that I mean I bow down to God for guidance in all decisions. I do not let my conscious mind make decisions. I ask God to guide me. This is how I practice obedience. To whom? Only to God, for I am a divine servant, vehicle and channel.

You too must practice obedience to God. Ask God to help you guide your life in the manner he has planned for your soul's fulfillment. This is so very important for your soul. Your soul has many more lifetimes to pass through. Your soul can be brought to the very highest realm and rest there for hundreds of human lifetimes on the time dimension. If you go to the highest realm, then God will give you a special duty. God may even send you back to take up a human lifetime or the lifetime of another form.

It is God who decides. God watches you, always, lovingly. God assigns to you duties during this lifetime and when you pass on. Therefore you can see that it is so very important to be listening to God. In this manner, you are living in divine relationship with God.

As you prepare to get out of bed, turn your first thought to God. "Dear my precious soul, we are to awaken on this morning with our thoughts only upon God and service." By saying these few words, your soul will now take over the purpose of this precious day. You will live this very day with your soul as the boss. You must realize that this is not always the case because often your ego, your logical head, makes the decisions. Your ego runs your emotions and you become imbalanced, even ill. Your logical mind can cause blockages within your body and your spiritual channels.

This is why it is so very important that only your soul is to be the boss. Secondly, as you awaken in the morning, you are to say hello to God. "Dear my precious soul, we are to awaken on this morning with our thoughts upon God and service only. Dear God, please be with me now. I bow down to you. I love you. I honor you. Please guide me through this day. Please help me to be kind and compassionate. Please help me to always think of others first. Please help my soul to purify further. Guide me and I shall obey. I am so very grateful. Thank you. Thank you. Thank you."

So what is the meaning here? Before I tell you, I ask you to feel your own body now. Are you tingling? Are you hot? Is there energy moving inside you? Is there golden light around you? Did you enter with me into the sacred space of prayer? Ask your soul these questions, and you will know how deeply connected you are with God.

I only bring you to the door. You must walk through it. The meaning here is that I give you the golden keys for your soul's journey. You do the work.

To connect your soul with God each day, begin with this morning prayer. It is essentially the main pipeline to God.

Now you can continue further. God is in everything. God is in nature. This is easy to see and understand. As you get out of bed, you wash your face. This water comes to you through the many rivers, lakes and oceans on the planet. This water comes to you through the falling rain in the sky. The clouds that make the rain that bring you the water, these very clouds abide in the heavens. Think in this manner as you wash your face and you will be closer to God. You will be appreciating the infinite connection between yourself and the entire universe.

As you move into your day, connect your soul with God in gratitude that you have a human body and have been given a human birth.
What is the meaning here? If you were not to have a human body,
you could not be reading this book. This means that having a human body gives you the possibility to hear these wisdom teachings
that feed your soul and allow it to grow. These teachings are food for
your soul.

Connect with God as you look up to the sky. Breathe in the breath
of the universe. Drink deeply of the energies of the sun and the moon.
These too are creations of God. Bring these energies into your lungs,
your body, your circulatory system, and you will receive the blessing
of rejuvenation. The ancient teachings of Peng Zu and Lao Zi carry
these divine blessings for the purpose of a long and healthy life. You
too can enter the channel of these teachings, and now, as I am a direct
lineage holder of these practices. In this moment, I bring you direct
blessings of this tradition. Think of these words in the middle of your
day, and look to the heavens, to the planets and beyond.

In this manner, your thoughts as well as your soul are living in divine relationship with God each day and throughout the entire scope
of your days.

Create in your home a sacred space that speaks the language of
your soul, the choices of your soul, the dedication of your soul to the
Divine. This space is personal to you and an expression of your soul.
Go to this space each day, at the beginning of the day and at the end.
Bow down to God. Give thanks for what you have received this day.

In this manner, you both begin and end your day with a deep
connection between your soul and God. The Soul World sees what

you are doing. The Soul World understands your intention and your dedication. In time, you will come to understand how this connection will transform your life while you are here on Earth.

In divine time, there is no time. What is the meaning here? In the emptiness condition, there is no time or space. In Heaven there is eternity. These are two ways to say the same thing.

So if there is no time, what is there? Only now. This means that you must apply all that I am teaching to you now. If you put it off and say, "I have to do such and such," this means you are not living my teaching. The moment of the "now" will pass, and so will the opportunity to bring your soul to the highest levels and rest in the divine heart of God.

This is much deeper than thinking to yourself, "I am merely putting something off until later." No. This is wrong thinking. You will miss the moment to jump into a completely new channel of existence. When I tell you "now," I am opening to you a doorway into living in a new dimension of divine relationship with God. It is a bit like a fast-moving train, and I am reaching out to grab your hand and bring you aboard. If you say, "Later, after I finish such and such," the train is gone and so am I.

I have already told you that we have met many times before. In a sense, we have met just like I described to you with the fast-moving train. Sometimes in life, there is only a moment available for you to make the jump necessary for your soul journey. The tugs and the push to remain in your old life as you have known it to be are very strong. Sometimes, the tug to stay where you are is so strong that you can totally miss this golden opportunity that I offer to you.

What I have shared with you just now is only the beginning of your soul journey as it relates to connecting with God each day. In time, you will ask God to guide you more and more. You will learn how to listen with your heart to God. You will learn many special abilities. But for now, this is where you begin.

Connect Your Soul to the Souls in the Universe

It is with great humility and deep gratitude that I am able to share with you this most special section in this book.

This era we are entering is known as the Soul Light Era. It is the beginning of our coming out of a time of darkness and moving further into the light. It is called the Soul Light Era because all souls in this era will be able to shine their light fully.

Bow down now! What I have just said is most sacred. All souls, can you image, all souls throughout the entire universe, galaxy and beyond, to all other dimensions and further still .... All souls that abide with you abide beyond the Milky Way .... All souls that abide beyond each star that itself opens to another universe .... All souls that abide throughout the dimensions of time and space .... Yes, my precious sons and daughters, yes, all souls will be able to shine their light.

This is an era of the greatest light imaginable. It is the era of light that will surpass the brightest lights of thousands and millions of souls all realizing enlightenment together, simultaneously! It is a light even beyond that!

Picture that light as it progresses through timeless and empty space. Picture that light touching the heart of each soul, everywhere, in 360 directions. This is how the Soul Light Era will shine. This is how the Soul Light Era will transform the entire creation that God has brought forth.

This is beyond your logical thinking. This is beyond the ability of your mind to understand. Do not worry for in time, not only will you understand, but you, yourself, will directly experience this! You will, in time, stand in the middle of this explosion of light. You will, in time, send your soul light out to every soul in the entire universe. And they will send it back to you until everything dissolves into pure luminous nothingness of God's divine grace.

In this manner, you will be living in divine relationship with all souls, everywhere and in every time.

Begin now with me, for I feel your hearts quivering and I see the tears in your eyes. Your soul so deeply yearns for this blessing, for the beautiful sweetness of bliss. Your gentle soul wishes this for all souls. Your beautiful soul is opening now in hearing my words. Yes, this is the space in the center of your heart that can open to love the entire universe. Yes, your heart is that big. Your love and compassion are that great. Open your hearts and connect with all souls for they too are longing for this comforting quality of peace, this quality of coming home.

Open yourself, open your heart, and hear the song of the universe singing to you now. It is so soft and sweet, coming from so far away. This is the celestial symphony of all souls in song. It is the song of the heart within all souls. It is both inside your heart, and your heart is the entire universe. Open, fully open. Close your eyes and rest, and let my soul show you this blessed union with the Divine and all souls.

How do you connect with all souls? You connect through your Message Center or heart chakra. Let your soul abide in the very center of your chest, the home of your heart chakra. Now, from this very center of your heart, you send out light. Feel it now as I speak to you these words. Feel the light in your soul, inside your heart, sending light out to the souls in front of you. Just shine. That is all, for the rest will follow.

Shine with your soul light, and you will feel the love that has been longing to come out from your own heart. Feel the gratitude as you expand your heart and let the love shine! It is such a welcome relief! You do not need to hide your love or your beauty! Let the love shine!

In this manner, you will be living in divine relationship with all souls. In this manner, you will be connecting with each and every soul in the entire universe, from the single soul in front of you to your family, your friends, your enemies, strangers, animals, plants, formless souls, souls of darkness, souls of light, lost souls, saints …. It truly matters not which soul or how many souls .... Just connect with your heart. Let the love shine from your very soul to others.

This most sacred teaching I have just shared with you can bring you through the door of enlightenment. Take my words most seriously, for it is not often that a spiritual master so generously and openly shares these secret teachings.

Speak to the Soul in Each Person

Your daily life must now move from that of being in the physical body and of the material world to that of being guided by your soul. So it stands to reason that if your soul is now the boss of your daily life, you will wish to speak with other souls in a similar manner. What is the meaning here?

It is most simple. First, your soul is now the captain of your ship. Your soul is the decision maker in your life. Secondly, your soul wishes the same for others. So your soul must now make a shift and speak with the soul in every person you meet. When you speak soul to soul, you will go beyond the logical mind and overcome any obstacles that are present between you.

To speak to each person's soul is to honor that person and to remind that person about the purpose of this lifetime. It helps the other person to wake up. So many people today think that material wealth will bring them peace and fulfillment. They need to wake up! You can help them by speaking to their soul. Look them deep in the eyes, and speak with compassion and understanding. Let them hear what a soul sounds like when you speak to them. A soul can recognize another soul immediately.

When you speak to another in this manner, you are doing a big service. When I teach as a spiritual master, tears come out. People cry. Why is this? Because I speak the truth and their souls know this, and they cry for it brings relief. This is also soul food. People are hungry for this. It is soul food, not material wealth, that will bring a meaningful and peaceful life.

I will give you a simple key to your daily life and your close relationships. Enter into prayer and call in the soul of the person with whom you wish to speak. "Dear soul of so and so, I love you and honor you. Please come here now so that I may speak with you ...." Continue to tell the person what is on your mind. However, a word of caution here: speak only in positive language and with respect. In this manner, you are speaking from your own soul and not from your ego.

For example, if your husband is jealous and wants more of your time than you are willing to give, then ask the soul of your husband to feel more fulfilled and happier. Ask that he feel more loved and secure. As your soul speaks in this manner, his soul will begin to balance his own emotions. The result is that he will be more secure and less needy of you and your time. You must always speak in a positive way to help the soul grow strong.

If you have a request for your career to grow, call in the soul of your boss or the person who can help this happen. I call this "soul marketing." Ask the soul of your boss to look favorably upon you, your performance, your potential, and to give you the chance to jump to the next level. Again, do this in prayer, for you are then calling upon Heaven's Team to help you.

I will give you a third example of speaking to the soul of another person – if someone begins to be angry with you because perhaps you did not do something that person wanted you to do. As they express their anger, let your soul begin to chant. Chant God's light or God's love quietly for two minutes. Watch. You will see the anger dissolve after only two minutes. Why is this? Because you are doing a great service. You are transforming the darkness of the anger into God's light and love. You are feeding the upset soul of the person in front of you with beautiful love and light. Their soul will feel it, and the darkness of the emotions will gradually pass.

Remember to always see the soul in each person. Understand that their soul is on a journey just as your soul is on a similar journey. Most likely your two souls have met before and there is unfinished business between you. This is an opportunity to clear the karma and learn the lessons for both your souls. This is a special gift for your soul and the soul of the other person. This is a form of unconditional service.

Honor and Cherish all Souls

To lead a life that has unconditional service for other souls is living in divine relationship. What is the meaning here?

To live in a relationship with the Divine is to manifest the highest purity, compassion, unconditional love, total devotion, universal service, humility, respect, commitment, forgiveness and light while humbly standing in front of another soul. To live in this manner is to completely cherish, embrace, and hold tenderly the soul in front of you. To lead a life where each moment within each day that you can possibly live is lived with these qualities emanating through your eyes and your heart is the highest and most pure way to live.

To "cherish" is to hold the soul of another as your baby. All souls in the entire universe at one time have been your baby, and you have been their mother. This is the true closeness between all of us. Open your hearts and feel closely now the eternal embrace of all your children as you bring them into the center of your chest. Open your heart as you hear my words and bring in the entire universe. Each soul in this universe is your baby and now is being held tenderly inside your heart.

This is the deepest meaning of living in divine relationship because of the total love and total wisdom of understanding our true connection. To be in this Oneness is deeper than the oneness of union joining all that is. To be in this Oneness has a love that is so sweet, so compassionate, so protective and so deeply blissful. This Oneness of bliss where we cherish the entire universe is the true returning to the Source, our home.

I am not merely describing to you the feelings of this wisdom teaching. I am showing you directly how to get there yourself. These are not idle goals to hear one day and forget the next. This is a practice to help you realize enlightenment in this single lifetime.

Honor the worm. One day I may come to you disguised as a worm. This is a test to see if you will cherish me and treat me with kindness when no one is looking. This test will let me see your true self, your diligence in your practice. I will see your heart in action. Are you kind? Are you forgetting your practices?

A worm has a soul. The soul of the worm may before have been your sister or your pet. You may hold a karmic debt to this worm that you can now settle by showing kindness. Think in this manner about all animals. Then think in this manner about all plants. If you must harm a plant, pray to the soul of the plant for forgiveness and then chant for the well-being of the plant. Give the plant thanks for the service of feeding you. Send more light to the plant. This is but one example of honoring the souls of plants and animals.

You must think in this way to further the journey of your soul:

- Your soul has several jobs to do in this lifetime.

- One job is to make peace with all souls.

- This may mean to complete that which was not finished before.

- This may mean to pay back a debt for some unkind act that you did in another life or this life.

- This may mean to learn a lesson that will help your soul realize a higher level in the Soul World.

- This may mean to see your enemies as friends who are showing you things you do not like about yourself that need to be changed and purified.

- If your thinking is a little bit off or "funny," you must purify your thoughts and return to honor and cherishing as your
golden keys to enlightenment.

Again I say to you, manifest only the highest qualities of which
I speak today, and live by those qualities as you address all souls in
the entire universe and beyond. In this manner, you will be living in
divine relationship with all souls.

Soul to Soul

Shining light abides as the essence of all souls. This light is around
each soul as a halo with different hues of light and color. This is the
rainbow body of the soul. As your soul reaches higher levels of enlightenment, the rainbow body becomes more brilliant in each color.
The rainbow body emanates more fully into space around the soul.

As your soul realizes saint level, your rainbow body can fill the
sky. You are then like a brilliant star that shines on a clear night in
the physical world. As a saint, your soul abides in the spiritual world,
shining out to other saints and servants of the universe.

The many rainbow bodies in the spiritual world shine in all directions, into all galaxies and even further, to other dimensions beyond
your conceptual mind. Where these brilliant iridescent colors touch
each other, there is born a pure soul of the Source that is called a
"light being." This is an immaculate conception of the rainbow light.
Within this pure soul is a golden funnel like a column that swirls
into another dimension. This swirling opening is a doorway to the
Divine. It is the task of this pure soul to attract all souls to its funnel

and then to move them through this swirling opening into the heart of the Divine.

How do I know this? Because this is where I was born. I was born when two rainbow light bodies touched each other with an electricity that shot out into the surrounding space, causing ripples that then touched other rainbow bodies. As these other rainbow bodies received this electric ripple, these other saint souls sent a quality of love and wisdom back to the Divine of the original point of connection. This all happened almost simultaneously. It was a flash of beautiful light charged with electricity.

I was then born as an awareness of the most pure rainbow light of many souls in the saint and heavenly realm. This birth of a pure soul came before my many physical lifetimes of many forms. I tell you of this now because the awareness and the wisdom that were given to me originally are my connection to this very day with the highest saints. This is also my connection to God, the original Creator of all light, movement, form and formless.

So when I speak to you on this day of "soul to soul," I am speaking of a connection that is of the highest realm in our universe. It is a soul-to-soul connection between the rainbow bodies of the saints. It has taken me time to lay the foundation for your understanding of soul-to-soul connection. I first had to speak to you about the soul within your physical body and how to connect with the soul in another physical body. I had to speak to you about the souls that abide in everything — animal, plant, stone, planet and on and on. Then, and only then, could we move to a higher level of soul to soul in the heavenly realm.

I hold each of you closely now as I open your minds to the possibilities of the universe and beyond. You are all precious to me, and I cherish and honor you.

Your job now is to continue to open, to purify your karma, to clear your thinking, to pass your spiritual tests. Then, and only then, can you truly understand the swirling golden channel that is a funnel to the Divine. Then, and only then, can your soul travel back to the Source, our home.

Transform Your Soul

Open Your Spiritual Channels

As the rose opens within the garden, so must you open to the Divine. As the rivers water the Earth, so must you water your soul. What is the meaning here? I speak to you of a rose and you understand. You have an image of a rose. I speak to you of a river and you have an image of a river. You are seeing with your Third Eye. This is the meaning here.

When your logical mind gets out of the way, I can surprise you and you will "see." This is my gift to you. My gift is to show you that you already can "see" with your Third Eye.

And if I were to tell you that your heart can hear the language of the heavens, you would not understand me. So I must tell you as simply as possible. Your heart chakra can listen to the universe. I call this divine "Soul Communication" because you are communicating with the Divine and all the heavenly realms. You can communicate with the highest saints and bodhisattvas. You can communicate with the entire spiritual world through your heart.

But you must learn how to open. When I speak of your spiritual channels, I speak of your Third Eye, your heart, and your entire chakra system. I also speak of your meridians. I also speak of your energy centers. This is your spiritual body. It is invisible to you, yet to me it has light of many colors. This is how I can read you and know how open you are.

Place your hands in the prayer position, now, as you are reading my book. Be humble and open yourself to my words. Good. Now we begin.

I am a servant, vehicle and channel of the Divine. I will bring to you many gifts that will further your spiritual journey. The gift I give to you at this time is that of Divine Connection. "Divine Connection" is a new ability that God has passed to me in this special year. In keeping with my teachings from my teacher, Master Guo, I must quickly pass on all that is given to me. So on this special day, I will transmit it to you through this page in my book, directly into your heart.

Prepare! Dear soul, welcome. You have been drawn to me and to my book because there are many messages for you to hear. The most special transmission I am about to give to you has never been done through a book. I "kai guang" each page with the living presence of God and the light comes directly to your soul.

Open your heart. Open further. Open …. ooooppppeeeennnnnn. I love you. You are my special daughter and my special son. Open your heart further. Let me touch you with my light. Feel the waves of energy moving towards you from the vastness of the universe. My light wave of love opens your heart.

Hear my words in your heart. Receive my message. Trust your mouth to open and begin to speak the message you receive. Let me borrow your mouth. Open. Trust. Speak out the message you receive.

I give to you the ability to open your heart to the Divine. With this ability, you will always be living in divine relationship with the entire universe and the entire spiritual realm.

Now say, "Thank you. Thank you. Thank you." Bow your head to show respect. Acknowledge your gratitude to receive this special gift of opening your heart to the Divine. Acknowledge your gratitude that this gift comes to you through my special book. This gift is hidden within this book, and you have found its most precious secret spot.

This gift is a golden key to opening all of the other parts of your spiritual channels. What is the meaning here? This golden key is so very special. It is the key of compassion. It is the key of hearing with the heart. It is the very center of your spiritual channel network. Without this golden key, your entire spiritual channel will only partially open. Your accuracy will not be very high. Many think they are open when in fact they are not. This is the importance of the golden key to your heart.

Knowing this meaning, I suggest that you bow down, place your forehead to the floor, and thank God for this special gift you have just received. If you are not comfortable doing this, that is fine also.

Next, use this golden key that is the ability to open your heart to the Divine by asking the question, "Dear God, How may I now open further my spiritual channels?" Listen, my lovely son and daughter, for the answer will be heard in your heart. Yes, I can open you further. But I wish for you that you learn how to do this for yourself.

That is another gift I give to you. I tell you to do it for yourself. I give to you the power to open yourself further. I place this power in your own soul. Now, do a good job!

"Dear soul of my Third Eye, open further." Yes, speak to yourself.

"Dear soul of my Zu Qiao, shine my light and use all my potential brain cells to understand this beautiful universe and its wisdom."

"Dear soul of my Lower Dan Tian and my Snow Mountain Area, together you are my very foundation. You stand between the heavens and the Earth. Help me to open further!"

"Dear soul of the heavens, and dear soul of the Earth, help me to open further. Place a lightning rod, a golden rod from the heavens, through me and deep into the Earth. May I always be an antenna of the light of the Divine."

"Dear soul of my heart chakra, my Message Center that hears the word of the Divine, I am so very grateful that you are my golden key to further opening. I so dearly wish to be at one with the Divine. I thank you many times. I bow down to you many times."

In this manner, and with these prayers and requests, you will receive further opening. In the receiving of this opening, you will increasingly be living a divine relationship with the entire universe.

Know also, my precious sons and daughters, that you will tremble as the power of my divine energy and divine light move through you. Be not afraid. It is a good sign. You are opening and your muscles must learn to relax and surrender. In time, there will be no more shaking. That time will signal that you are now an open vessel for God's work.

To transform your soul while you are in your physical body and living in the physical world is the work you have begun. Opening your spiritual channels is the first step. With this step, you are now ready to enter an entirely new world, the world of all souls of all times and of all directions.

Pass Spiritual Tests

My precious sons and daughters, I have given to you secret teachings that before have only been passed between a spiritual master and a single disciple. However, in this Age of the Shining Soul Light, the time is most urgent to bring forth my mission: that of bringing enlightenment to all souls in the entire universe, light and dark sides together. For this reason and because of this timing, I have taken a vow to share everything that I know. I have also taken a vow to share each blessing as soon as it comes to me. In this manner, I am but a funnel of divine wisdom directly from the heavens to your soul. This is why I so generously and freely give to you what I know.

In this precious book, I have spoken to you of the essential wisdom, the alignment with the Divine. I have given to you precious gifts as well. Now I must pass to you the struggle, the pain, the lessons that will come to each of you. These struggles are opportunities to grow, yet they will be most painful.

The pain may last for days and weeks. For in truth, the greater is your potential service, the greater will be the struggles placed in front of you. I call these "spiritual tests" because it is the spiritual world testing you to see how deep your commitment is to your soul journey. It is also testing you to see how strong you can be, how pure you can be, how dedicated you can be. For to serve God and the divine mission of bringing enlightenment to every soul within the entire universe, you must be strong, so strong that nothing, no one, no event, no thing can sway you from the path of your true purpose in this lifetime.

There is a second reason you must go through serious spiritual testing. This reason is to open your heart to deeply feel the pain and anguish that others go through. Your heart must have compassion that is so pure and deep that you are gentle and wise with all souls. You must personally know what their struggles are like so that when you teach or serve others, you can truly say you understand.

There is a third reason for spiritual testing. In your past lives, there have been lessons that you failed to complete. There have been lessons that you did not know how to complete even if you wanted to and tried very hard. There have been lessons that did not have the opportunity to come to you because your life ended too soon. All of these lessons must be learned and completed for your soul to be whole and therefore holy. To pass successfully into the Kingdom of Heaven or the Pure Land of the Buddhas — whatever spiritual teachings you follow — to pass into these higher realms, your soul must have suc-cessfully mastered the condition of humanity and its lessons.

There is a fourth reason for spiritual testing. You must prepare to teach others. Other souls will look up to you for guidance and sup-port. To show them the way to total purity and enlightenment, you must know the way yourself. You must gain their respect by speaking with an honest and straight-forward manner that will tell their souls you understand, you have mastered the struggles, you have found the way through the testing, and you can therefore guide them. This is a service that can be offered only after you complete all spiritual tests.

There is a fifth reason for spiritual testing. It is to burn the nega-tive karma you have accumulated over thousands of lifetimes. Until this negative karma is fully removed, you cannot receive the complete impact of my blessings and transmissions. What is the meaning here? This means that when I bless you and empower you, you receive a partial result. This also means that for me to complete my mission, that of bringing enlightenment, body, mind and soul to you, I must first clear your karma. It also means that for you to be of service to others, your karma must be clear. This is most important.

Within spiritual testing, there are several "gates" that represent a level of spiritual struggle that is beyond the realm of human struggle. Your soul must pass through Hell's gate, the sex gate and the power gate. What is the meaning here?

The gate of Hell or monster gate is where your spiritual channels are open enough and you are sensitive enough that you can see, hear, feel and know the presence of monsters and the dark nature of the universe. You must face the monsters with compassion. You must welcome them and ask them what it is they wish and why it is that they have come to you. You can then learn how to help them transform into light. This is a very high level of service.

The second gate is that of sexual desire. The most beautiful, youthful and seductive male and female deities and souls will dance before you, enticing you to fall into their trap and wander off the purpose of your soul's journey. They are reflections of gods and goddesses that dwell in your mind and in the minds of all humankind. They represent that which you have longed for and never succeeded in fulfilling. Therefore, they are the embodiment of passion and desire and lust. They also have great power that abides within their lower energy centers. It is a power that can help you to grow if you can master their seductiveness and continue on your journey.

The third gate that is part of spiritual testing in the realm of the Soul World is the gate of power. Power in the physical world can corrupt any man or woman. Power in the spiritual world is far greater and far more lethal if it is abused. As you grow spiritually, there are many enticements beyond the sexual one just mentioned. These enticements can mislead you and you can fall into a darkness, an abyss that is as deep as your soul has managed to grow in height or expansion. If your soul level is very high, your fall can be just as far going down.

I am speaking of powers to heal, to gain riches, to bring soul abilities, to give blessings. While each of these powers has a side in the light, it also can have a side in darkness where it is abused. These powers of manifestation can seduce a spiritual master to leave his or her own path. This gate of spiritual testing on the topic of power is a big discussion. I can only mention it briefly here and hope that you remember my words and my warning. I dearly hope for you that you can find your way through these three gates.

So whether you are in the human realm or in the spiritual realm when the testing comes, the way through is always the same: remember that this is a test. This is not easy, for part of the nature of testing is that you are so trapped in your mind that you do not recognize this as a test. Secondly, ask yourself a key question: what am I to learn here? Remember this is an opportunity to learn and to complete that which was not finished before. And lastly, let it go, be unattached, be forgiving, be pure and glide smoothly through in a state of peacefulness and equanimity.

In this manner, you can be living in divine relationship with pain, struggle, darkness, monsters, sex, power, and incomplete tasks of prior lifetimes. How, you may ask, is this possible? How can all this negativity be part of living in divine relationship? You may think that purity has nothing to do with darkness or evil.

Indeed, there are some teachings where this separation is taught. Those teachings say that purity and light are one thing, and darkness and evil are another. Yes, this has a truth. But you must go deeper if you wish to truly understand and realize enlightenment.

The deeper truth is so beautiful and it is most simple. The Source knows neither good nor evil. The Source embraces all and everything. The Source is where true and complete enlightenment abides.

The Source is beyond the spiritual world. So to realize my complete mission and to help you also realize the true purpose of your soul, you must learn that darkness and light are one and the same. This is deep wisdom I give to you now. This is how you can make friends with, and even harness, the dark side.

To live in the awareness of divine Oneness is living in divine relationship with all and everything. There is nothing more complete than this.

Clear Your Karma

My most precious children, I speak to you today as a divine servant, vehicle and channel to bring you truth and guidance on your soul's journey. This is my duty. This is my honor.

I use these words most carefully. I use the word "children" because it carries with it a guidance for you. This guidance is that your soul is like a child in its innocence, and purity, and joy. Your soul may be ancient and wise. Yet your soul enters this life with a hope and a freshness that is the juice, the very immortal nectar, that will carry you through your journey. It is this child aspect of your soul that will pick you up as you go through the spiritual testing. It is this child aspect of your soul that will allow you to experience so much that is beyond your ordinary thinking. This is why I speak to you with the word "child."

"Precious" is so very important. As you read my words, let yourself truly and deeply feel how very precious you are to me. There is no other one like you. You are a perfect and unique flower in my eyes and in the eyes of God. As you grow and open your spiritual channels, you too will see your own flower in your heart. When you see this, you will know that my words are truth. You are precious.

Feel your own preciousness. In this manner, you are reconnecting with the most extraordinary gift of all: God gave you this life. That is why you are precious. As you feel your own preciousness, you are opening to deeply receive the gift from God, the gift of this life. Sometimes it is hard for souls to love themselves as God loves you and as I love you. You must allow this love to flow. Then you can feel your child nature, your joy, your hope. And most of all, you can feel loved.

This that I am describing is your natural state. Within this natural state are those qualities of the highest nature possible for a human being: purity, compassion, wisdom, patience, equanimity, and peace. In this natural state, your soul shines with oh, such a beautiful light. This light shines from your heart in the very center of your chest. This is your soul light shining in the Soul Light Era. You belong here. You belong in this natural state in this Soul Light Era. This is perfect for this lifetime.

So when I speak to you about transforming your soul, I am telling you that your soul has a natural state such as what I have just described. While you read my words, your soul is resonating with all these beautiful qualities. You may even have tears come to your eyes. You know this is true. And, even more deeply, you yearn to live in this natural state.

This yearning is a hunger, a magnet bringing you through the spiritual testing, bringing you through the gates, and bringing you closer to your original state. Yet it has been many lifetimes since you were in that state. This may surprise you. You may think with your logical mind that when you were born, you were totally pure. Yes, it did appear that way.

The purity, however, was not very deep because as you grew up and got older, many struggles arose inside you and around you. This is your karma ripening. It takes time for the karma that you were born with to ripen and show itself.

Karma comes in with your soul. It is an aspect of your soul, for it is the record that is carried throughout your many lifetimes, whether you were a human, or a plant, or an animal. This karmic record ripens in this lifetime. The ripening of the karma means that an issue or a particular pattern of struggle repeats itself until you finally learn how to overcome it.

I will give you a simple example. If your spiritual master gives you a task such as writing a book, you must complete this task. Why? It is far deeper than just obeying and being respectful. Your spiritual master can read your Akashic Records and knows exactly what you did not successfully learn in your prior lifetimes. So when you are given a task, this is an opportunity to pass a spiritual test that you have failed before. It is most difficult to do this because the same karmic threads that caused you to fail before are even stronger now. They gained power when you failed in your past life. So it takes greater effort on your part to successfully pass the test in this lifetime. Your teacher knows all of this, and carefully gives you many opportunities to complete the task.

There are many types of karma cleansing to help your soul return to its natural state. To complete a task is only one example. This is a big journey and it is hard work. Do not think that the spiritual journey is easy, for it is not.

A second type of karma cleansing can be accomplished by paying a debt. This debt is to another soul or souls whom you have harmed in a past life. You can do this through prayer and by asking forgiveness. A compassionate spiritual teacher can also help you by paying the debt for you. Here the virtue that the teacher has accumulated can be given to you so that that virtue wipes clean your debt. In the physical world, money talks, but in the spiritual world, it is virtue that talks.

A third type of karma cleansing can be done when you offer service to others. If you offer service without any hope of payment or reward, this is the proper attitude. This is true service, and it will bring you your own virtue that, in turn, will help your karmic record. If the service you offer is silent and you speak not of what you have done nor take any acknowledgement for it, this kind of yin service has the greatest value and will bring you even more virtue.

A fourth type of karma cleansing is to successfully go through spiritual testing. You must view hardship — be it in terms of your finances, physical health, relationships, emotional balance or whatever else — as a blessing in disguise because this attitude will help you welcome the process that, in turn, will aid in the transformation of your soul.

A fifth type of karma cleansing is not in any way related to past lives. It is the clearing of your karma in this life. Even though you may come to me to receive my virtue and to wash away the darkness that clouds your soul, there are many things you can do that bring the very same darkness back again. I will help you out of my generosity and my dedication to bringing many souls to enlightenment in this very lifetime. Yet I can help you only so far, and the rest is then up to you.

This is most important. I give you my blessings. You are the one to receive them as deeply as you can. This part is your work. Do not think that just because I clear your karma, you are done. It is not like that. Yes, in that moment, on that day, I can tell you your karma is cleared. But if the very next day you do something that brings negative karma to you, then you are beginning to accumulate new karma.

So if I give you a task, that you now understand is both a spiritual test and an opportunity to clear past karma, and you do not accomplish it .... oh my, my heart goes out to you. Now you understand the deeper implications and meanings in my teaching.

And lastly, I will tell you how karma works at the time of your death. In the spiritual world, there is one special department with a head saint and many workers. In this department when you die, they gather the information from your Akashic Records and from this current lifetime to see where you are on the balance sheet. Your record of services has one side for good deeds and positive karma, and it has one side for negative deeds or bad karma. The two sides are balanced at the time of your death. It is as simple as that. The result of the balance sheet determines where you go after you die. It also determines the level of your soul. It is, as you might say, "the bottom line."

As I have told you many times before, "There are no secrets in the Soul World." You need to embrace what comes to you with a positive attitude and an open heart. For this attitude is the one that will best assist you as you transform your soul's darkness and move further into the light that is your true nature and your natural state. To truly live in a divine relationship of any kind, your karma must be clear.

Clear Your Thinking

Karma carries with it patterns of thinking. Some think this is the ego, which is also true. But I want you to think more deeply and to see that my teaching on past lives is not only related to the external deeds or acts we committed that move with us when we die. There is a much more subtle level: our thinking.

Over many past lives, we develop a pattern or a habit as to how we view our lives. This habit becomes a pattern of thinking. Each thought in turn produces an emotion or a feeling. This feeling then leads to an action. You can see that merely looking at the action as the root of karma is not complete. You must look to the habitual thinking pattern of the soul.

As the karma ripens when you age and go through years of your life, your thinking pattern becomes more apparent. People around you begin to anticipate how you will respond because your habits are now more strong and rigid. Your perspective about how the world is and more than that, how the world ought to be, gets louder. People see that.

Your conceptual mind comes not only from this lifetime or from your ego, but from many lifetimes and many failed spiritual tests. So you have much to overcome in this life if you are a serious student. If you are smart, you will see how big this opportunity is for your soul.

I tell you many times to go beyond your logical thinking. You may hear these words and think I am only saying to open your mind to new experiences and deeper wisdom. That is true. I am also saying that. However, I am saying much more. I am telling you to break free from your karmic way of thinking. Break free! Break the bonds of your past!

Your thinking must become purified, fresh, spontaneous, open. Your thinking must reflect the emptiness that has no position and receives the exaltation of God without any limits! Your thinking must explode into all directions and beyond all limitations. Your thinking is your consciousness that reaches out into the many heavenly realms to receive wisdom teachings. Your thinking is a funnel through which enlightened knowledge of the universe, its origins, its future, all relationships of understanding can flow without being impeded by any pattern or perspective. The unknown is vast and beyond any boundaries. For you to enter into the unknown and receive, you too must be free of any obstacles that will stop this divine flow and divine connection.

It is therefore your thinking that must live in divine relationship with the true Source. This is not possible. Yet this is all there is and can ever be. Your thinking must now embrace both the impossible and the ultimate truth. Open your mind and both will live inside you. Your mind must be able to hold paradox.

I have already taught you this, only on a smaller scale. I have told you that the light and the dark are as one. Now I tell you that thinking any word limits your mind. And yet you must be able to enter into the space of no space where there is no thinking and no "I."

You must therefore not only purify your thinking, you must bring your thinking into a place of clarity in which there is no thought, just awareness. And stay there, for it is here that you will bring all paradox, all light and dark, into one single truth. This is the Source. This is beyond even God, who is still a thought in your mind. When the thought of God moves inside you into a total Oneness where there is no distinction between you and God, then, my precious sons and daughters, we are there together.

This is the heart of God that bursts open into infinite light and love. It is peace and bliss. It is both empty and beyond nothingness. This is the true Source, the true home of your soul. I am but the vehicle and channel from the Source coming to guide you home.

Open to Your Life Purpose

Yes, yes, I say to you gently, yes. This lifetime, you can come "home."

Home is where you already are. Home is where I am. Home is where God is. Home is everywhere. Home is a quality of oneness and bliss that is so very sweet and kind. It is familiar to you. This is the purpose of your life, to come home and abide in the very essence of Oneness.

I tell you clearly: your life purpose is the journey of your soul to enlightenment. Yet the quality of enlightenment I have yet to teach because many so far have not been ready. Now, perhaps, on this most special day, you are ready.

Open yourself now. Open your spiritual channels. Open your heart to hear the Divine in my message. Place to one side your pattern of thinking. Place to one side your logical mind.

You are ready. It is possible in this single lifetime for you to clear your karma, to pass your spiritual tests, to align with the Divine and your Shi Fus, to connect with every soul in the universe. And having done all of this, you are now ready to come home.

Home is beyond soul enlightenment. Soul enlightenment merely opens the door to the vision of the magnificence that is possible. Body enlightenment is taking each and every cell within you and giving it the purest light possible. In this manner, each cell with maintain its youth and thus give you many more years to accomplish what your life purpose is.

Mind enlightenment will bring you to the highest understanding of the principles of the universe and you will directly experience all galaxies and all time as both beyond space and time. You will increasingly enter, and maintain in your daily life, the highest quality of the buddhas and saints that is possible. Your vision of clear light, your vision of luminosity and energy, your vision of God and the heavenly realm will no longer be merely glimpses or visions. Your vision will be embedded within every second of your life, and you will be transformed into a pure being of light and love to bring universal service to all souls.

You will enter the Source directly and live as an expression of this divine state of Oneness that each and every religion seeks to pay homage to and yearns for throughout all time and all cultures.

It is within the natural flow for you to continue to open in this manner once the process is clearly understood. Your God nature or your Buddha nature or your natural state, however you wish to call it, is already present within your soul. My job as a divine servant, vehicle and channel is to further your journey upon this road with this goal of final and complete enlightenment.

At this point we can no longer say you are living in divine relationship because you are the living embodiment of the Divine. Your eyes will sparkle with light and energy that is boundless. Other souls will see this, and you will give them hope that they too, each and every one of them, can achieve and realize the space of the living embodiment of the Divine. This is your natural heritage. This is also a gift from God. This is also a gift from your spiritual master. Honor each and every one well.

Be inspired! Be uplifted! For I am giving you the golden keys to enlighten your soul!

Purity, Service and Compassion

Only a Clear Mind Can Be with God

A clear mind is like a diamond, multi-faceted, reflecting only pure light rays in all directions. A clear mind is polished and cleansed of all defilements and impurities until it reaches its final stage of diamond.

A clear mind began as a dirty rock in the earth, covered with mud and insects and excrement. To become clear the rock had to be washed well, even scrubbed, so one could see its rock nature. Then it had to be rubbed with sharp instruments until its skin of dust and dirt was removed. The rock's soul must have cried out in pain to have its dirt removed. The rock's soul did not want all this rubbing and washing. It wanted to stay in the cool, dark earth, a diamond in the rough.

The rock's soul had no aspirations to be with God. It was quite comfortable being just a rock in the ground as it had been for many lifetimes. At one point, it had even been a boulder until it was shattered by an earthquake many millions of years before. But deep in the ground as a rock, it was content. In its soul was a process already occurring that was purifying on the inside. But this was not in the awareness of the rock, for the rock had no awareness, being a rock.

I am like the master of the diamond mines and many of you are like the rock deep within the earth. I know your light. You only sense your light. It is my job to remove the dirt and the dust, to scrub you until the diamond purity begins to shine through from the inside. This is part of my job.

Your mind starts out like the rock and transforms into the diamond. Your mind has great potential, far beyond your logical thinking.

First of all, I tell you that your mind is not in your brain. Yes, your brain has great potential because only twenty per cent of its cells are in use. That is why your logical mind, which is located in your ego, cannot figure it out. It is too small. I am not talking here about your ego, nor your brain. I am talking about your mind, which is a part of God's mind.

This mind is the diamond in the rough. It is located in your heart, in your Message Center. This mind must become clear and shine light to all souls, as I have previously described to you.

This mind, the diamond mind, must become pure in thought, in emotions and in karma. Then, and only then, can your mind join with God in a divine relationship.

How, you may ask, can you do this? I will tell you. There are three parts involved: thought, emotion and karma.

To become pure in thought, pay attention to your thinking. Catch yourself when you have a "funny thought." By this I mean any time when you complain, blame, think ill of your teacher or of any other soul. When you catch yourself doing this, quickly apologize and ask for forgiveness from that soul and from God as well. Then change your thought to a positive version of whatever you were busy destroying in your mind and ego. Work very hard on creating open and positive thoughts. This will help you to transform your external world as well.

Secondly, pay attention to your emotions. When you have negative thoughts, dark emotions will quickly follow. When you are stressed and anxious, look to your thoughts and change them. Then your emotions will change as well. It is necessary to have a balanced heart with balanced emotions to create a pure mind in your heart. You must learn to become "rock solid" centered and peaceful so that no matter what I throw at you, you remain peaceful. This is one way that I test you.

Third, your karma needs to be cleared, for your karmic imprints are located in your heart. Your heart is the very vessel that must become as crystalline pure as a diamond.

So far, I have spoken of the need to gain purity. How do you do this? One key is to offer unconditional service to all souls and to God. I have described to you how to do this already. Just let me add that "unconditional" means putting yourself to the side and doing the work of the Divine.

To be asked to give service is a gift to you. Do not think it is a gift you are giving to others. Wrong already! God is giving you a gift, an opportunity to gain greater virtue, to forget yourself, and to enter the space of golden light that comes with the act of giving service. God is giving you a key to walk into the golden light!

So I am telling you clearly that the golden keys are purity, unconditional service and compassion.

Compassion comes only partly through effort. It is true that you can try to be more compassionate. But the quality of this form of compassion is more like surface empathy. It is like playing "nice nice." True compassion is felt in your heart. Your chest feels like it is ripping open to give birth to a space big enough for the entire universe to enter. You must go through serious spiritual testing to feel this deeply the suffering of others.

Then your heart is listening to God, listening to all souls who sometimes sing of joy and sometimes sing of sorrow. Your heart hears all and has compassion. Then you are entering the state of purity and clean mind that a true servant of God must demonstrate.

When this quality of compassion is genuine, other souls will see it and know it to be real. This quality of compassion is inspiring to other souls and they will wish to be as you are and to shine as you do. This is another form of service, for you are leading by example and inspiration. This is also part of my teaching, "If I can do it, you can do it."

These qualities of clear mind, diamond purity and reflection, unconditional service and compassion, are essential to entering into living in divine relationship with God. Anything shy of this is obscuration. Remember, when you are in spiritual testing, your mind is not

clear. You are in the process of karma cleansing and must successfully pass through this step to enter the state of clear mind.

Beyond Logical Thinking

I almost laugh here when I think of my close students. I watch
them and give them plenty of room to do their "trip" or play at their
"role." They are not easy to manage! They are such characters! So I
give them lots of chances to just do what they do.

They, each and every one, revert back to their prior life experiences and try to apply those to my teachings and my tasks. They fail
each time, and they do not know why. They want to run my organiza-
tion as if it were a physical world business, but it is a spiritual world
business that they do not understand. They want to use their experience, but really they want to impose it upon something so new that no
one has ever heard of it!

They come as very skilled professionals and yet want to impose a
small framework onto something that is beyond their logical thinking.
It takes them a very long time to see the impossibility of this! This
becomes one of their first spiritual tests. They must let go of their own
logical thinking to work with me. It is no different than the letting go
I have had to do. In fact, I make it much easier on them, than it was
on me, and continues to be on me.

They do not understand the deep spiritual principle that is obedience. Obedience to whom? It is not to me, but to God. I must be
obedient to God. I am a direct channel to God. I hear and follow
God's guidance to me and to my mission on this Earth at this time. So

when my close students and disciples try to argue with me, they are going against the guidance I am told to follow. This is very serious. I am a very serious master and must help my students understand the mistake they are making in their logical thinking.

Yet, they grow so fast spiritually. They develop the abilities of their soul. They begin to discover the depth of my words, "beyond your logical thinking," and inside, they simply let go. In that very act of letting go, they are practicing detachment from their old ways.

They also go through so much struggle, testing and blessing. They know the pain of the spiritual journey. Being born into your true nature, your deepest connection with God and the entire heavenly realm is not easy. Many cannot make it. They must cling to their logical thinking.

Logical thinking will tell you many messages, especially when you are in a period of spiritual testing. Your logical thinking moves through life in a linear fashion, but the spiritual world has 360 degrees! And that is only in this dimension. Just think about that. How can your thinking be accurate when only one or two or three degrees can be seen from the perspective of your logical thinking? You are blind. That is the simple truth.

So my job is to open you, to assist you by lifting you up into the blessings of the Divine. I cannot do that when your logical thinking says, "This is crazy." You will only fight with me and disagree. I can see you fighting me in your mind even when you do not tell me. Be-

PURITY, SERVICE AND COMPASSION

cause I am a spiritual master, I can know your truth even when you are not open with me.

That is all right. I have compassion for your struggle. I had my own struggle. I went through so much — doubt, fear, loss and even a crazy mind — to the point where my family cried for my safety. They saw my struggle. That is how it goes.

Your family may think you are crazy too when they see you changing. It is only human nature to be afraid when you see family or friends changing. That is the real crazy part: people want you to be happy and yet they are afraid when they see your joy or the light in your eyes. They have to deny it because of their logical thinking.

I tell you this because your logical thinking will trap you and get in the way of your true life purpose. Yet do not think that your logical thinking is bad. It is doing its job. It has a purpose in the physical world. It is a language that is necessary. Even in the spiritual world when it is blocking you, it still has a purpose. What is the meaning here?

Your logical thinking causes you struggle. That struggle is the face of your karma. You must come to see clearly again and again your deepest struggles and the thinking that goes with them. Until you see your own thinking, you cannot learn the lessons you must learn to grow spiritually.

So I am saying that your logical thinking must be used correctly. It is a mirror. Look at it. Hear your thought. Go to the very root of such thought, be it in this life or another. Go to the karma of that thought and cleanse it through prayer or ask for my blessing. Pull it out by its roots, make peace, forgive where you need to, and let go.

When you do this many times, you will see that your logical thinking is a tool that leads you to clearing your own karma. Then there will be more space inside you. A peacefulness will come. You will be better prepared to follow Divine Guidance through obedience that is smooth and filled with gratitude. This is the other side of the coin.

Always remember that there is a purpose to the dark side or the side that is negative and filled with struggle. It is up to you to find how to quickly move through it and reach the other side. Both sides have a purpose. Together they are one.

I have spoken with you thus far about what logical thinking can do inside you. Now I will teach you what the word "beyond" means on the spiritual journey.

Beyond. Go beyond. Go far and then go further. The soul has no limit as to how far into the universe it can travel. The soul can travel beyond this universe. The soul can travel beyond linear time. The soul can travel to a place where light and sound were once one. The soul can travel to Heaven. The soul can travel to the realm of Hell.

The soul can travel when you are dreaming. The soul can do a job at night when you are sleeping. The soul can subdivide into many souls and go in many directions, doing many jobs simultaneously. The soul can go to the heart of God. The soul can go into the emptiness. The soul can go to the Source of all creation. The soul can travel into another soul. There are no limits to where the soul can go.

Beyond. Go beyond. Just as the soul can boundlessly travel, so can the soul have many boundless abilities. The soul can call upon any saint to heal any cell and any organ within the human body. The soul can call upon any soul in the physical world and have a conversation that will be heard and will change the very core of that relationship.

The soul can call upon God to be the voice of God when writing or speaking out loud. The soul can simply be quiet, waiting for the inspiration and guidance of God to enter and to tell it what to do next. The soul can bring golden light into any room and to any body. Truly, it is boundless what the soul can do.

This begins to give you a sense of what "beyond" can mean in terms of soul travel and soul work. There is yet another aspect of "beyond." When your soul enters emptiness, you are on the edge of going truly "beyond." Some ancient traditions call it, "gone, gone, gone beyond."

This is because in the emptiness — where there are no distinctions, no good, no bad, no you, no non-you, where there is no direction or time or sound, where there are no points of reference or attachment to concepts — in this true state of emptiness, you are on the edge of vastness beyond comprehension, bliss beyond expression, love beyond separation.

It is from this emptiness that wisdom teachings arise.

As you arrive here, you are truly living in divine relationship. Allow your heart to rest in this place of no place. Rest with ever so subtle awareness that has no thought and no "I." Rest as quietly as you can as if suspended between breaths. When the power, the energy, the visions, the teachings suddenly open to you, still continue to rest and suspend yourself as long as possible.

This is beyond your logical thinking: out of nothing, you are taught something that has great wisdom. What is the meaning here? I will tell you simply this truth: I go into the "empty state." My guidance as well as my blessings and teachings all come to me when I enter the empty state. I give myself totally to God and to universal service. I am a divine servant, vehicle and channel. To do this job I must be empty and enter the hero condition of total emptiness for the words of the Divine to pass through me. This is the deepest meaning of "beyond": to enter the emptiness and go beyond.

Offer Unconditional Universal Service

If your soul quivers with what I am about to tell you, then you are totally one with me in spirit and you understand my mission: to bring enlightenment to all souls in the entire universe.

There is one position only that completely reflects what I mean by "living divine relationships," and that is the position of a true servant. The meaning here is that your soul totally dedicates your life to serving other souls throughout the entire universe, all dimensions and all times. This is taking a vow that moves both forward and backward in time. This vow will radiate throughout your entire family and all generations, past and future, and this will change their lives and their karma.

To be a true servant, you must be pure, cleansed of past karma, keeping only positive thoughts and kind words for others. You must focus solely upon how you can alleviate the suffering of others. You must focus upon others and not upon yourself. You must offer service to both the light and dark sides, to monsters, to demons, to hungry ghosts, to saints, to animals, to plants, to rocks, to stars, to the moon, to the sun, to your enemies, to your family, to your friends, to souls that have no form, to the sky, to all thoughts, to all light, and most of all, you must offer service to the Divine.

What is the nature of the service? This will change each lifetime and each year and each day. Service will be placed in front of you as an opportunity. It is up to you to see the opportunity and take action when it is there in front of you.

Inside there must be the proper attitude, always, whether an opportunity is present or you are quietly alone. This internal attitude is one of humility and deep quiet. Humility is the reflection of no ego and no attachment. Humility is the recognition of your place in the universe, both how small you are and how connected you are with the Oneness.

Quiet is the state of no thought, no stress, no complaints. It is a peaceful state. From this attitude of peace and quiet, you are more able to listen with your heart. Your heart is your Message Center, from which you both hear and speak with the Divine. To be a universal servant, you must always be in this state of quiet and peace to listen well and receive guidance.

How you can serve each day will change because that is a universal principle, the principle of change. You must be flexible as you serve. Be not attached to how you served yesterday. Always be open and listening to how to best serve now.

I am telling you here how to live in divine relationship in your daily life. This is a basic teaching for you to apply wherever you are and however you live. It is an internal attitude you can cultivate.

Externally, your actions can take many forms as you think of the well-being of others. Be a universal servant with your children, your spouse, your parents, your friends. Be a universal servant to your work colleagues, your clients, your peers. Be a universal servant to the beggar on the street corner.

How can you do this? There are many ways. I will tell you a few. You can use your mind to creatively find many other ways. For example, when you see struggle between strangers, chant God's light. When you hear of disasters, war, poverty on the news, ask in prayer for light and love to replace anguish and turmoil.

Pray in this manner in the morning when you get up. Pray in this manner before each meal. Pray in this manner throughout the day. Always give thanks for what you have. Always ask that the virtue you gain through helping others be given to other souls. Take nothing for yourself. Whatever comes to you as teachings and wisdom, always quickly pass on to others.

These are but a few of the many ways you can serve throughout your day, wherever you live, and however you live, things that you can do for others as a universal servant.

If you are a rich person, tithe to the poor. If you have wealth of land, tithe to the homeless and build them shelter. If you have an abundance of material goods, give these objects to those who have no bed or blanket or comfort. Give in this manner, quickly and quietly. Give directly to those who need. Give not through large groups or impersonal contact. Give face to face, anonymously.

This, and only this, is unconditional giving. Meet the eyes of the receiver and hold warmth in your heart.

Be not afraid to enter the streets of the poor, the displaced, and the foreign. When you are on a divine mission to give, you will always be protected.

To live each day with this purity, obedience, flexibility and commitment to being a universal servant, beyond any condition, this is truly living in divine relationship with God.

Open Your Heart to the Entire Universe

To open your heart to all souls, to care for them and about them is only a small aspect of the meaning of my words. The deepest meaning here is that your heart contains the entire universe. That is the quality of an enlightened heart. That is the ability of a highly developed soul.

My prayer for you as you read my words is that your soul drink deeply of the soul food I am giving to you, and that as a result, your soul grow and realize a high level of development.

My prayer for you is that you realize soul enlightenment and that with this, you continue further on your journey. Soul enlightenment is only the first doorway.

My prayer for you is that you open your heart, open your compassion, open your deepest caring for others. With this quality of love and kindness, you will begin to be of true service to others.

Without this depth of true caring, you can offer only empty tools and spend time without substance. However, when you do care, do love, do feel kindness and wish to cleanse all the wounds of others, then, and only then, are you entering the doorway of true compassion.

Inside your heart lie many abilities of the soul. When your soul abides in your heart, your soul level is ready for this next step. Inside your heart is a center I call the "Message Center" or "Communication Center." What is the meaning here?

This Communication Center can both send and receive messages from all souls, all saints, and the Divine. You can hear with your heart. You can speak from your heart. You can speak the words of saints and God from your heart. When you move aside, the voice of God will flow through you. You can have a conversation with God.

You can also have a conversation with any soul in the entire universe. In this manner, you can heal other souls and their relationships, careers, and any life issue.

When your soul level is of high standing, you can bless any soul from your heart. There are many abilities and powers your soul can manifest when you are pure and being of universal service.

All of this is one small part only of what your heart can bring to this universe. The deepest spiritual wisdom here is that your heart can hold the entire universe inside it. What is the meaning here?

At this time, I am one of the few servants, vehicles and channels of the Divine who has this special ability while still in human form. There are many high spiritual souls, saints, bodhisattvas, deities who have this ability, but most of them are in the Soul World. In this physical world, I am one of the few. Yet because of my generosity and because of the task in front of me, I will quickly bring my advanced students, disciples, and you as well to the soul level where you have the ability to bring the entire universe into your heart.

This is a gift I can give to you when you are ready. Study well my books, apply my words, ask for my blessing to help you prepare.

To open your heart to the entire universe is to be a saint of compassion. Sit quietly now. Bow humbly before the Divine. In the very center of your chest rests your heart, your spiritual heart. It is a beautiful flower waiting to open and unfurl into space. Feel each petal opening and stretching, beautiful, happy, free. Breathe deeply and continue to let each beautiful petal stretch even further into the vast blue sky, into the infinite reaches of the universe.

Feel the pulsing of your heart. Feel the life force beckoning to the universe. Feel the souls that are invisible and far out in the sky responding to this flower's scent and love. Feel the connections coming towards you as these souls approach. Open further and the entire universe will live and shine and radiate its joy from inside the center of your chest. Open further and feel the flood of all the souls coming into you in joy, each carrying its own light.

All these souls sit down within your heart, expectantly waiting for your words of love and peace to uplift them and assist them on their own journeys. Feel the unity of all souls. Feel the joy and the love. Feel the hope and the light as all these souls seek a universe of soul enlightenment. Welcome all the souls into your heart. Bow down to them and show them your humility, your strength, your compassion.

This is how you begin to welcome every and all souls into your heart. This is how you begin to share and to teach. This is how you offer the deepest service as you bring each soul into your heart and into its own soul enlightenment. As you do this, you are living in divine relationship with my mission to bring universal soul enlightenment in the Age of Shining Soul Light.

When I give you a gift like what has just been done, always say, "Thank you. Thank you. Thank you." This is a thank you to the Divine, to your teacher and to your own soul. You are blessed on this day. You have received a very high teaching.

Conclusion

Each moment is divine.

To live in divine relationship with God, your Shi Fus, your spiritual master, all saints and all souls, and with your own soul requires a total alignment within the golden light channel emanating from the Source.

Within this golden light channel is pure emptiness, emptiness that is beyond time, beyond space, beyond any dimension. It is the opening to the Source. Within this timeless dimension there is only this instant, this now, this moment. That is all there is.

Therefore, to live in divine relationship with the Source, there is only this moment.

When all is in perfect order, this moment is a golden funnel that will carry you directly to God, to the heart of God, to the soul of God, and to the Source that abides within the soul of God.

This gift of connection with the Source and the soul of God is present for you each moment of your entire day. This gift of connection is present for you wherever you are and however you are. This gift of connection abides within your own heart.

Remember this.

I give you the golden keys. I give you my deepest blessing. I give you my wisdom.

Remember this.

Live with purity, service and compassion. Live within this moment. Align yourself. In this manner, you will always be living in divine relationship.

Remember this.

With my deepest love and sincere wish for your total enlightenment,

Zhi Gang Sha

Acknowledgments

From the depth of my heart and soul, I humbly bow to my teacher and spiritual father, Master Zhi Chen Guo, to the great enlightened masters, and to the Divine, for bringing me these gifts of Heaven's Library. Without these blessings, without this guidance, I would never have had this opportunity to be of universal service in this way.

The teachings in this book must be followed and honored, for they are the teachings passed down over many thousands of years from teacher to disciple. They offer simple daily wisdoms that will connect your soul with the Divine, with the very heart of God. For this profound connection, I humbly bow down to God.

Again, I cannot honor my teacher, Master Guo, enough. For he has brought me through the door between Heaven and Earth, opening my spiritual channels and pointing the way. I humbly bow down to my spiritual father, Master Guo.

I thank my editors for their support, long hours, and great efforts to assist me in bringing Heaven's Library to the public. I thank my students for their love, care, compassion in bringing Heaven's Library to the public. I tenderly hold each of you in my heart. I thank my wife and children for their understanding of this journey and the many ways they support me and this task.

I thank the soul of Heaven's Library for bringing the brightest light directly from God unto these written words.

About Master Sha

Master Sha is an MD from China, a traditional Chinese medicine doctor in China and Canada, an extraordinary healer and a divine master.

The best-selling author of Power Healing, Sha has been featured by the Public Broadcasting System as one of the most powerful qi gong masters in our time. He is also the First Disciple and worldwide representative of Master and Dr. Zhi Chen Guo of China, the founder of Zhi Neng Medicine and Body Space Medicine.

Master Sha's teachings emanate from a lineage of Buddhist and Taoist spiritual wisdom thousands of years old. His own powerful contribution is to make these teachings simple, practical and accessible to anyone who wants to embark on a journey of healing and self-realization.

Master Sha is a direct channel for the Divine and a vehicle to offer divine service in Mother Earth and the universe. He has three missions in life:

- to teach healing, to empower people to heal themselves and others

- to teach soul wisdom, to empower people to enlighten their soul, mind and body

- to teach universal service, to empower people to become unconditional universal servants. Universal service includes universal love, forgiveness, peace, healing, blessing, harmony and enlightenment.

About Heaven's Library

Heaven's Library is an ever-growing collection of deep wisdom that Master Sha is delivering for the Divine on a vast array of topics, ranging:

- from healing the psyche in the Soul Light Era to reincarnation as a divine teacher,

- from conscious parenting to divine messages from the planets, stars and galaxies,

- from ancient and indigenous healing wisdom to contemporary Soul World events.

These teachings are the harbinger and early treasures for the Soul Light Era, a 15,000-year period that began August 8, 2003. In this age, many of the greatest known saints, bodhisattvas and other holy people are slated to re-appear, many of them imminently.

The Soul Light Era will be the time of soul over matter, of soul-to-soul communication with all souls, and of the discovery of the path to essential and divine Oneness.

Heaven's Library provides a beacon of true wisdom for all on Mother Earth in her transition time into the new era.

Visit www.heavenslibrary.com to view the current online offerings. Come back often as more and more wisdom pours through.

Additional Resources

Master Sha offers free remote healing every Tuesday and Thursday evening via teleclass. The list of healing and blessing miracles reported on his website grows weekly. Please register at www.drsha.com.

Visit the online store on the website for details of Master Sha's books, CDs, DVDs, audio- and videotapes, Divine Downloads, retreats and certification programs currently offered.

Be sure to register each week for the free Soul Healing Water.

About the Cover

The images on the outer border are symbols of the petals of the lotus. Around the entire border are fifty-four petals, on both the front cover and the back cover, making a total of 108 petals. One hundred eight is a most sacred number, as it represents the total number of realms of Heaven, from which the wisdom, knowledge and practice of Heaven's Library emanate. Jiu Tian (the "nine heavens") has nine primary layers. Each of these layers has twelve sublevels, for a total of 9 x 12 = 108 sublevels. The border also represents the subtle layers and levels of soul transformation. It is in subtlety that the greatest transformation of the soul occurs.

The images on the inner border are a symbol of the sun and a wave. This combined image of the sun and a wave represents the balance of light and liquid, yin and yang, sacred fire and sacred water which purifies the soul, mind and body. The placement of these symbols in the four corners represents the four directions. From all directions, the knowledge and power of the Divine are gathered and concentrated into the golden urn.

The golden urn, a deep, wide bowl, is symbolic of Heaven's Library. The three legs symbolize the three highest powers of the heavens: the golden power, the rainbow power and the purple power. The flames carry the sacred wisdom and knowledge that the soul will receive from, as well as the aspect of soul consciousness that will be uplifted by, the precious treasures within the book. The flames represent the fire which burns away all blockages to reveal the truth. The flames also represent the ignition of inspiration through truth. The purple flame on the left is in the position of guardianship. The rainbow flame on the right is in the position of nurturance. The golden flame in the middle is in the position of new creation and growth.

Upon the body of the golden urn is the inscription:

Wisdom   Knowledge   Truth

Below this is the following:

Place within all emptiness and ignorance and be filled with the sacred wisdom and knowledge of Divine Truth.

This inscription serves to remind the soul that sacred wisdom and knowledge are Divine Truth. Divine Truth can only be acquired when the soul opens its heart and enters into emptiness, which then can be filled with sacred wisdom and knowledge. When the soul cannot open its heart, the soul remains in the state of ignorance and is incapable of receiving sacred wisdom and knowledge. When the soul opens its heart, the soul must enter into the state of emptiness, for if the heart is filled with attachments, there would be no room for the sacred wisdom and knowledge.

The seven golden balls signify the seven houses of the soul for humanity.